澜沧江—湄公河农业合作发展报告 2020

Report on the Development of Lancang-Mekong
Agricultural Cooperation 2020

农业农村部对外经济合作中心　编著

中国农业出版社
北 京

图书在版编目（CIP）数据

澜沧江—湄公河农业合作发展报告 2020 / 农业农村部对外经济合作中心编著. —北京：中国农业出版社，2021.12

ISBN 978-7-109-29209-3

Ⅰ.①澜… Ⅱ.①农… Ⅲ.①澜沧江－流域－农业合作－国际合作－区域经济合作－研究报告－2020②湄公河－流域－农业合作－国际合作－区域经济合作－研究报告－2020 Ⅳ.①F333

中国版本图书馆 CIP 数据核字（2022）第 040179 号

澜沧江—湄公河农业合作发展报告 2020
LANCANG JIANG—MEIGONG HE NONGYE HEZUO FAZHAN BAOGAO 2020

中国农业出版社出版

地址：北京市朝阳区麦子店街 18 号楼

邮编：100125

责任编辑：孙鸣凤

版式设计：王　晨　　责任校对：沙凯霖

印刷：北京通州皇家印刷厂

版次：2021 年 12 月第 1 版

印次：2021 年 12 月北京第 1 次印刷

发行：新华书店北京发行所

开本：700mm×1000mm　1/16

印张：12.75　　插页：4

字数：260 千字

定价：128.00 元

澜沧江—湄公河农业合作发展报告 2020

Report on the Development of Lancang-Mekong
Agricultural Cooperation 2020

编委会

主　　任：隋鹏飞　张陆彪

副 主 任：韦正林　李洪涛

委　　员：刘　江　王先忠　刘翔洲　姜　晔

主　　编：李洪涛

执行主编：王先忠

副 主 编：姜　晔　王秀东

编写成员：祝自冬　张　斌　徐佳利　臧良震

　　　　　闫　琰　谭光万　高延雷　韩昕儒

2016 年 3 月，中国在澜沧江—湄公河（以下简称"澜湄"）合作首次领导人会议上提出设立澜湄合作专项基金项目，在 5 年时间内提供 3 亿美元支持澜湄流域六个国家的中小型合作项目。农业是澜湄合作五大优先领域之一，在澜湄基金的支持下，各成员国实施了政策对话、产业提升、能力建设等类型农业合作项目。

澜湄基金农业合作项目的实施显著促进了澜湄农业合作的发展。项目支持澜湄六国农业部门建立了多层次和多主体交流对话平台，推动了战略对接、政策交流和经验分享；支持水稻、天然橡胶、特色果蔬、渔业、畜牧业等重点产业的技术交流合作，推动了澜湄区域农业产业提质增效；支持共建农业技术培训中心，开展境内外培训交流，提升了澜湄区域农技人员的综合能力。

为综合评价澜湄基金农业合作项目对澜湄农业合作支持促进作用，本报告将对澜湄基金农业合作项目实施以来的典型案例进行梳理，并在此基础上归纳分析项目的主要模式、做法和成效，进而展望未来澜湄基金农业合作项目的规划设计方向，为进一步有效利用澜湄基金等资源，促进澜湄农业合作可持续发展，提高澜湄合作项目实施成效和质量提供科学依据。

编委会

2021 年 11 月

目 录 CONTENTS ///////////

I

总报告

澜湄农业合作项目概览

2016 年 3 月 23 日，澜湄合作首次领导人会议在海南三亚成功举行，会议以"同饮一江水，命运紧相连"为主题，柬埔寨、中国、老挝、缅甸、泰国、越南六国领导人宣布正式启动澜湄合作，共同建设面向和平与繁荣的澜湄国家命运共同体。会上，中国提出设立澜湄合作专项基金，拟在 5 年时间内提供 3 亿美元资金以支持澜湄六国的中小型合作项目。2017—2020 年，澜湄基金陆续支持了近 400 个项目；农业是澜湄合作五大优先领域之一，各国累计实施农业合作项目 100 余个。

澜湄农业合作项目围绕柬埔寨、中国、老挝、缅甸、泰国和越南六国的农业发展需求，通过加强农业政策对话、农业产业提升、农产品贸易投资促进、能力建设等领域合作，实现了成员国之间更加紧密的农业交流，实现了互促共进。项目在推进农业资源保护与利用、提高各区域粮食安全与食物营养水平、推动落实联合国 2030 年可持续发展涉农议程、实现乡村振兴和共同发展等方面做出了积极贡献。

一、澜湄农业合作项目简况

2017—2020 年，澜湄基金累计支持实施农业合作项目 100 余个，其中，湄公河国家实施项目近 70 个，中方实施项目近 40 个。项目涉及的农业领域呈现多元化特征，涵盖种植（水稻、橡胶、香蕉、咖啡、果蔬、木薯、竹子等）、养殖（山羊、蚕等）、种子、加工、病虫害防治、农产品贸易、农村发展与减贫等多个领域。

2017—2020 年，中国农业农村部组织实施澜湄基金项目近 30 项，主要围绕澜湄农业支持体系建设、多领域平台搭建、重点产业（包括水稻、橡胶、渔业等）技术示范、农业生产基础设施建设以及技术人才培训等诸多领域开展合作。

二、澜湄农业合作项目主要类型

已经实施的澜湄农业合作项目主要包括政策对话、产业提升、能力建设三种主导类型。

（一）政策对话主导型

政策对话主导型项目旨在建立多层次、多主题交流对话机制，进而推动技术、产业领域务实合作，最终实现澜湄区域战略对接、政策交流和经验分享。具体做法包括搭建和升级政策对话平台、组织有关交流活动等。

实践过程中，根据参与主体的不同，政策对话主导型项目主要做法如下：

一是合作支持体系建设。项目以政府部门和农业科研院所为主体，以澜湄农业合作中心为依托，以维护澜湄农业合作机制正常运转为基础，通过打造农业技术、投资、贸易等领域合作交流平台，发挥各国比较优势建立农业合作支持体系，为实现国家之间农业合作互联、生态资源互通、经济资源互助提供战略支撑。已经开展的农业合作支持体系建设项目，一方面，支持保障了农业联合工作组机制运行，为各国农业政策沟通、农业发展战略对接与设计搭建了沟通桥梁；另一方面，构建了"智农澜湄"信息推广平台，实现信息发布、农技推广、专家问答、农民交流论坛等功能，为各国农业技术、信息本土化推广构建了服务平台。该项目支持澜湄六国农业部门、地方政府农业部门、重点企业和研究机构建立良好的合作关系；与此同时，通过组建专家团队，为进一步推进澜湄农业合作奠定坚实基础。

二是区域全方位农业合作。项目以媒体宣传为基础，以电视节目为媒介，通过打造多国主流电视媒体合作平台或联盟，积极宣传澜湄六国在农业方面的科技知识和发展经验，促进多方实现媒介交流。已经开展的澜湄区域全方位农业合作项目以各国媒体为桥梁，积极传播澜湄流域各国的农业科技、农村发展、农民生活等多方面信息，逐步实现"看"以致用。现已改编制作电视节目《中国农场》60期，拍摄制作《中国农场》新节目

32 期，制作《中国农场——澜湄行动》系列双语宣传片 6 部。节目宣传有效促进了中国与湄公河国家在农业领域的交流。

（二）产业提升主导型

产业提升主导型项目重点支持咖啡、水稻、天然橡胶、特色果蔬、渔业等澜湄区域特色优势农业产业的发展。具体做法包括：开展产量与质量提升项目，共建优良品种试验示范基地、技术促进中心、科技合作示范园区，构建农技推广与信息交流平台、生态养护交流合作机制等。

实践过程中，产业提升主导型项目主要做法如下：

一是通过建立试验示范基地实现产业升级。通过建立试验示范基地，对农业技术、优良品种、管理模式进行试验示范，带动当地农业产业提质增效和转型升级。典型项目包括：缅甸咖啡产量与质量提升、澜湄橡胶树栽培技术及加工示范基地建设、澜湄热带农业产业合作示范区等。其中，澜湄热带农业产业合作示范区项目，通过在柬埔寨建设 1 000 亩①椰子产业合作示范基地，实现合作双方在技术、管理、标准等方面的共同提高。

二是通过人员培训实现产业提升。通过在农业领域开展生产、管理、销售等多方面的技术培训，提高农业从业人员技能水平，提升当地农业生产经营软实力，间接实现产业提档升级。例如，缅甸咖啡产量与质量提升项目、澜湄橡胶树栽培技术及加工示范基地建设项目均开展了人员培训活动，有效地推动了农业产业的提档升级。其中，缅甸咖啡产量与质量提升项目在缅甸钦邦、克钦邦、掸邦、曼德勒省和马圭省进行了 14 次专业的咖啡生产培训，累积培训学员 1 639 人，极大提升了当地人员的技术水平。

三是通过保护生态实现农业可持续发展。通过在农业生产中推广绿色生产技术、加强生态保护监管、开展农业生态保护交流等途径，提高区域生态保护能力，促进农业与生态协调发展，实现农业可持续发展。例如，澜湄次区域水稻绿色增产技术试验示范项目以绿色增产技术的应用和推广来促进农业生产绿色发展。通过建立澜湄流域渔业和水生态养护交流合作机制、开展中老联合执法暨增殖放流等，水生生物保护及渔业合作项目显

---

① 亩为我国非法定计量单位，15 亩＝1 公顷。下同。——编者注

著促进了澜湄流域水生生物资源养护。

（三）能力建设主导型

能力建设主导型项目以传授农业专业技能知识为导向，着力提升澜湄各国农业官员、专家、技术人员、青年骨干等人员的技能。具体做法包括：建设农业技术培训中心、举办各层次人员培训活动、推动农业领域人才交流等。

实践过程中，能力建设主导型项目主要做法如下：

一是农业专业技术人员能力提升长期项目。项目通过双方合作建立农业生产基地，开展农业生产和技能培训，最终培养一批懂农业、会经营、善管理的农业技术人员。例如，澜湄流域国家农业产业管理与技术培训班，通过建立椰子产业合作示范基地，在进行农业生产的同时，对农技推广人员进行培训，极大提高了参与人员的农技水平。

二是农业专业技术人员培训班短期项目。通过在农业专业领域开展讲座、实验、考察等教学活动，实现澜湄国家之间的技术交流、成果示范、企业推介、经验分享等。例如，跨境动物疫病实验室诊断检测技术培训项目、沼气技术培训班项目和农药风险管理研修班项目，均是借助短期培训的方式促进专业技能提升。

三、澜湄农业合作项目实施成效

自澜湄农业合作项目实施以来，柬埔寨、中国、老挝、缅甸、泰国、越南六国通过共同努力，各国政府、科研单位、企业与农业经营主体通过多方联动与探索实践，完善合作规划，加强务实合作，在澜湄合作专项基金支持下实施了一系列惠及民生的农业项目，合作程度逐步加深，合作领域逐步拓宽。总体而言，澜湄农业合作项目在合作机制构建、技术交流合作、人力资源赋能、产业合作创新、区域福利共享五大方面取得实效。

（一）完善澜湄农业合作机制体系

现有合作项目主要通过以下两种方式建立并不断完善澜湄农业合作的支持体系。

一是完善多层次交流合作机制体系。项目建立包括政府机构、科研机构、各领域专家与技术工作人员等在内的多层次、多领域机制架构，就澜湄国家政策对话、技术交流、能力建设、信息交流、联合研究等合作事宜进行联络、协商、决策,落实澜湄合作农业联合工作组工作计划。依托湄公河次区域各国丰富的农业资源禀赋,合作构建澜湄农业发展优势区,探索开展农业项目合作,充分利用澜湄地区的农业资源,实现农业资源优势互补,提升农业综合生产能力。

二是加强宣传,深化务实合作理念。澜湄六国的农业生产方式与科技水平存在差异,各国文化也有显著不同。通过加强澜湄国家之间的媒体宣传合作,加大澜湄农业合作理念传播力度。例如,针对科技类和致富经验类选题,改编制作多档农业节目,并拍摄记录政府、农企等行动主体在湄公河国家的政策和活动。一方面,帮助各区域的农民了解并掌握切实可行的务农技术,以及项目落实程度与实效,有助于深化区域农业合作理念;另一方面,增强澜湄区域国家人民对澜湄合作项目的认同感,有效推进了澜湄区域国家的文化交流,为农业联通、民心相融奠定基础,有助于保障澜湄合作体系覆盖的广度与深度。

(二)深化技术交流合作

一直以来,科技、教育与人才交流是澜湄区域重要的合作领域。澜湄各国通过开展农业技术领域的交流与合作,构建技术合作研发平台,建设技术试验示范基地,带动了农作物优良品种、技术和农机、农资在澜湄国家的推广和应用,可以概括为以下四大领域:

一是粮食作物的技术交流与合作。定期召开项目推进交流会,及时掌握项目开展情况,提高执行效率。例如,澜湄次区域水稻绿色增产技术试验示范项目,通过开展水稻品种、技术引进试验,组装和推广适合当地大面积应用的水稻绿色增产技术,实现了周边国家水稻生产的绿色增产增收。

二是特色作物的技术交流与合作。通过实施橡胶树栽培技术及加工示范基地建设项目,示范并推广了橡胶园高产高效综合栽培管理技术,为澜湄各国科研院所、生产单位和农户提供技术指导。依托缅甸农村发展与蔬菜种植技术提升项目,开展蔬菜栽培技术交流活动,为蔬菜产业高效高质发展提供了技术支持。

三是经济作物的技术交流与合作。通过开展香蕉种苗繁育平台建设和标准化种植示范，收集、保存、评价柬埔寨本土香蕉资源，筛选优质及特异香蕉资源，为后续品种改良提供育种材料。依托澜湄薯类加工技术与装备研发平台项目，极大促进了中国和老挝、越南、缅甸等国家薯类加工产业的发展。

四是渔业领域的技术交流与合作。通过实施澜湄水生生物保护及渔业合作项目，针对考察和观测过程中相关鱼类所需的专业性技术进行定向培训，同时，对濒危水生物种实施更为有效的保护措施，提升了各国对水生生物的保护能力。

（三）完善人力资源培育体系

澜湄区域农业的发展离不开科技，更离不开人力资源的支撑。在信息和人员交流方面，主要以交流活动、论坛、研讨会等形式开展。以提升经营农业的业务素质和知识为导向，通过具体项目的直接落实，实现人力资源赋能，构建人才培养体系，进一步强化了澜湄国家间的农业交往，为澜湄农业合作提供坚实的人力资本支撑。

一是通过技术培训提高人员专业技能。例如，以澜湄流域国家热带农业人才培育工程建设为主体，举办多期澜湄流域国家农业产业管理与技术培训班，对澜湄国家农业管理官员、农业技术专家和涉农企业管理者组织培训。培训内容主要涉及有害生物疫情监测防治、农产品质量安全、热带经济作物生产加工、农业产业园区与农业信息化、热带畜禽养殖与饲料种植等。一方面，将符合"资源节约、增产增效、生态环保、质量安全"等要求的优质绿色高效技术模式进行宣传推广，提升了技术推广人员的专业技能；另一方面，通过开展培训班，提升了从业人员在不同领域的知识水平，将产学研紧密结合，并以此为纽带促进相关研究成果共享与传播，使得澜湄各国从业人员在获得相应专业知识的同时，还能够取得巨大的项目效益和影响力。

二是通过建立科技示范基地提升人员专业生产能力。农业科技示范基地成为集示范展示、技术指导、农民培训等多种功能于一体的农业科技示范服务平台，对全面提高澜湄国家的农业技术水平、促进各国农业发展有重要作用。例如，通过建设澜湄橡胶树栽培技术及加工示范基地，提供橡胶树栽培和加工技术培训，提升了当地橡胶生产专业水平。依托澜湄国家人力资源合作开发体系建设，注重基层农技推广人员能力素质提升和知识更新，极大地推动了基层农技推广队伍建设，提升了澜湄各国基层农技推广能力。

（四）推进农业产业合作创新

现阶段，澜湄产业合作类项目呈现集群化发展趋势，强化产业技术交流，创新农业产业合作形式，为推进产业提质增效起到了重要作用。与此同时，生态保护项目的实施，促进了产业绿色、高效和可持续发展。

一是通过保障经济社会效益，实现多行业高质量发展。澜湄农业合作项目涉及水稻、荞麦、薯类、天然橡胶、豆类、香蕉、椰子、胡椒、香茅草和渔业等多个领域，充分利用了澜湄国家农业资源和技术的比较优势，带动澜湄国家农作物的规模化、标准化、高效轻简化种植，产品质量和品质得到有效提升。同时，生产成本明显减少，农户和生产企业的抗风险能力增强，各区域产业优势更为明显，为保障经济和社会效益奠定了坚实基础。与此同时，多个项目同步推进，有助于"以点成面"确保预期效益的持久性，为澜湄各国农业领域的产业提升发挥重要的促进作用。

二是通过技术交流与合作，形成以技术为突破口的产业提升新模式。澜湄农业合作项目多数以技术合作为突破口，然后从技术合作逐步转变为农业全产业链合作，实现产业转型升级。例如，澜湄次区域水稻绿色增产技术试验示范项目，通过引入中国成熟的育秧、栽培、水肥管理和病虫害绿色防控等技术，形成试验示范基地与稻田综合种养模式。项目有助于实现传统产业生产、销售和管理模式升级，进一步促进农业产业化的发展，并加速实现农业现代化。

（五）实现澜湄区域福利共享

澜湄农业合作项目打造了政策、投资、技术等多种合作交流模式，覆盖种植业、养殖业、加工业、农业技术等多个领域，为发展福利共享和一体化结构奠定了坚实基础。

一是区域发展带动当地农民增收。澜湄农业合作项目通过提高各地区农民农业技术水平，为农民增产增收提供了技术保障。例如，应用推广澜湄次区域水稻绿色增产技术，引进、试验和筛选品质优、产量高、抗性好、适应性强的水稻新品种，为澜湄次区域水稻提质增产提供了种质保障。通过改善农产品产量和品质，增强了该区域水稻的市场竞争力，显著带动区域农民增产增收。通过建立政策体制机制，为农民增收提供了决策保障。由于项目从基层发起，农业管理和科技人员能够通过项目基地深入了解农业和农民的发展境况，为更好获取当地农户利益诉求、促进农业交流合作提供决策依据。

二是区域发展带来经济福利。通过推动农业产业的规模化和标准化，提升了农产品的质量和效益。澜湄热带农业产业合作示范区项目借助"企业＋农户"的现代订单农业经营模式，实行品牌战略和产供销一体化，提高产品质量并降低市场成本，增强产品市场竞争力；形成规范化的管理体系，进行统一标准管理、物资供应和品牌经营，打造了大型绿色农产品生产基地。同时，项目培育具备国际竞争力的农业产业和企业，促进农业产业走向标准化和产业化，提升农产品的国际竞争力，促进农产品的国际贸易。

三是区域发展带来生态福利。项目实施中注重农业生态保护、推动农业投入的减量化和绿色化生产，提高了区域生态环境保护力度，有效减少了对生态环境的破坏。此外，通过打造"生态保护＋农业开发"相结合的农业合作开发模式，既促进了当地农业产业的发展，又保护了当地的生态环境。农业可持续发展理念在澜湄各国得到极大认可，生态效益显著，为长期有效合作奠定重要基础。

四、澜湄农业合作项目规划设计方向展望

澜湄农业合作应在继续加强各国政策对话的基础上，立足农业技术深度合作，不断延长产业链条，带动各方企业合作，促进农业投资贸易往来，推动澜湄六国农业可持续发展。

（一）新形势与新挑战

在澜湄基金的支持下，柬埔寨、中国、老挝、缅甸、泰国、越南的合作和交流不断加强，在农业政策对话、产业提升、能力建设等方面均取得比较显著的成效，对区域经济、社会发展以及人民福祉等做出了重要贡献。但是，随着项目的深入实施，项目格局发生显著变化，合作领域呈现纵深发展。同时，受新冠肺炎疫情的影响，未来项目实施过程中也将面临

一些新形势与新挑战。

一是合作领域亟待拓宽。当前,项目主要以农业产业技术的交流合作为主,通过技术的试验示范及技术培训等方式来提升各国农业产业发展的技术水平,从而促进农业的高质量发展。但随着技术的逐步推广,各国农业技术水平不断提升,在立足于农业技术深入合作的基础上,农业合作项目应向农业全产业链方向发展,覆盖生产、加工、贸易等多个领域;同时,增加农业投资、生产管理、生态保护等多方面的合作,增强澜湄各国农业合作韧性。

二是可持续发展方面有待增强。现阶段,农业生产已不再是以获得产能为主要目标的传统生产模式,而是转向农业与自然环境协调的可持续发展路径。当前澜湄农业合作已有部分项目关注农业生产与环境共同发展,以及水生生态和渔业可持续发展领域。在全球粮食及食物系统受到新冠肺炎疫情和自然灾害冲击的形势下,确保粮食和食物安全成为澜湄农业合作项目实施的重要目标。因此,在未来的合作中,应加强农业可持续发展方面的合作,以农业生产与自然环境协调发展和区域粮食、食物安全为主要目标,保障澜湄区域农业可持续发展。

三是疫情影响下国际合作交流受阻。在新冠肺炎疫情大流行的背景下,国际合作交流面临着新的形势与挑战,澜湄农业合作项目也不可避免地受到新冠肺炎疫情的影响。从澜湄农业合作项目实施过程中遇到的困难来看,一方面,疫情造成人员、物资跨国流动受阻,聚集性实地活动几乎全部搁置,技术交流与培训活动受到严重影响;另一方面,国际投资贸易等活动因疫情影响进度缓慢,贸易成本和贸易壁垒增加,尤其是物流、仓储和检验检疫等时间和费用成本上升,各国贸易和投资难度加大。

(二)新方向与新举措

经过一段时间的积累与总结,澜湄农业合作项目取得了显著成效,产生了一些值得借鉴的经验做法,但仍需要抓住新机遇、借助新举措来促进澜湄农业合作高质量发展。

1. 新方向

一是拓宽农业合作领域。进一步拓宽农业合作领域,从农业生产端向农业综合发展的方向进行,既涵盖农业的生产,又涵盖农业的加工、销售等多个领域。同时，也要增加农业与其他产业融合发展方面的合作，如"农业＋休闲旅游业"等。

二是加强与其他部门合作。结合各国农业发展的薄弱点，加强与水资源、环境等其他领域澜湄项目的合作，增加农业基础设施投入以及配套服务供给，为深化农业合作、促进经济发展奠定基础。推动各国农业科研机构进行深度合作，联合研发适宜各地的生产技术、生产方法及创新管理模式，建立多方科研机构长期合作机制和人才交换培养机制。

三是增加传播的新媒介。建议增加澜湄农业合作互联网等新媒介平台，完善线上交流、线上与线下相结合等多渠道交流模式，同时加强各区域互联网基础设施建设，为农业合作提供新途径和新方式。

四是以保障粮食安全为重要纽带。积极推动澜湄农业合作，为保障各国粮食安全、解决各国食物供给风险问题提供帮助。

2. 新举措

一是加强农业政策对话。加强澜湄六国农业部门之间的政策对话，深化产业组织合作，建立健全农业领域投资、合作等相关法律制度，营造开放包容、互利共赢的农业产能合作环境，围绕农业领域加强政府和企业之间的政策对话。同时，各国政府要做好管理、引导和服务工作，营造公平竞争环境，大力扶持龙头企业，在财税、政策等方面给予优惠待遇，进一步增进传统友好，优化澜湄区域农业合作体系，为参与合作的国家和人民带来实实在在的利益。

二是拓宽农业产业链条。立足区域农业优势，充分利用各方市场和资源的比较优势，把坚持农业合作开放作为基本方向。在现有合作的基础上进一步拓展农业产业链条，深化农业产业上、中、下游的合作与发展，不断加强多双边农业国际交流合作，更好地为区域农业和农村经济发展服务。

三是加强农业投资贸易。利用国际投资贸易，实现区域优势互补。针对澜湄区域内的差异化市场，推动农业博览会等重大农产品投资贸易推介活动的组织和实施。同时，以此为契机，搭建区域内企业洽谈平台，推动区域内具有地域特色的农产品不断拓展境外市场，加强企业交流合作，提高区域特色农产品的影响力和知名度，拓宽农产品进出口渠道，促进农业投资贸易健康发展。

四是深化农业科技合作。深化多方合作，共享农业合作成果，以科技力量推动区域农业发展。继续依托科研院所、创新型企业和科技中介组织，建立农业技术交流合作服务平台，加强农业科技交流合作，深化在农作物种质资源保护与利用、作物栽培育种技术、植物保护等领域多双边合作。同时，推动区域农业联合实验室、示范基地共建，积极搭建产学研平台，促进产学研一体化推动区域农业发展。以此打造澜湄区域农业合作新格局，为未来农业合作项目的稳定实施保驾护航。

II

典型案例

第一篇 | 政策对话类

案例一　澜湄农业合作支持体系建设项目

一、项目目标

农业是澜湄合作的五大优先领域之一，澜湄合作启动五年来，在农业政策对话、产业发展、农产品贸易与投资、能力建设与知识分享等方面取得积极进展。2019 年 1 月，澜湄农业合作中心成立，作为澜湄合作机制下继水资源合作中心、环境合作中心、全球湄公河研究中心之后成立的又一中心，连续多年实施澜湄农业合作支持体系建设项目，充分发挥澜湄合作农业联合工作组常设机构和区域性支持协调机构作用，支持澜湄农业合作机制运转，开展澜湄农业合作规划研究，协助谋划和推动实施"丰收澜湄"项目集群，建立完善澜湄农业合作支撑服务体系，支持澜湄农业合作在机制完善、项目实施、规划研究等方面稳步发展。

二、项目活动

（一）支持澜湄合作农业联合工作组召开机制性会议

2017 年 9 月，澜湄合作农业联合工作组正式成立并有序运行，成员国轮流主办年度工作组会议。2019 年 6 月，澜湄合作农业联合工作组第二次会议在柬埔寨暹粒召开，柬中两国代表团团长联合担任会议主席。2020 年 10 月，澜湄合作第三次农业联合工作组会通过视频方式召开。

（二）推动建立澜湄农业合作支持机构

2019 年 1 月，澜湄农业合作中心在中国农业农村部对外经济合作中心正式设立。2019 年 8 月，澜湄合作农业科技交流协作组成立。2020 年 6 月，澜湄农业合作广西分中心成立。

（三）开展澜湄农业合作规划研究

2020 年 1 月，澜湄农业合作中心牵头起草的《澜湄农业合作三年行动计划（2020—2022）》于澜湄合作第五次外长会期间正式通过，成为澜湄合作农业领域的首个指导文件。澜湄农业合作中心自 2019 年起开始组织编制《澜湄农业合作发展报告》，定期梳理澜湄农业合作的进展、成效和经验做法，供澜湄六国农业部门及相关机构交流参考，2021年3月底，首部报告以中英双语的形式由中国农业出版社正式出版发行。

（四）协助开展澜湄农业合作项目管理

协助组织开展澜湄基金中方项目申报和实施，定期跟踪了解项目进展情况，及时提出相关建议，促进项目深入开展。探索解决农业项目规模小、领域分散、协同性不够、延续性不强等问题，提出实施"丰收澜湄"项目集群的工作建议并得到采纳认可。

（五）建立首个次区域线上农技推广与信息交流平台

整合各方农业科技资源、市场信息，构建澜湄农业技术推广与农业信息共享的农业综合服务平台（"智农澜湄"手机App），将中国先进的农业实用技术和农业信息服务模式转移输出，创新湄公河国家农业信息服务手段，增强澜湄区域农业政策交流、信息共享与成果转化。

三、取得的成效

（一）完善澜湄农业合作机制建设，打造次区域农业协调联动体系

澜湄合作农业联合工作组在推动澜湄各国政策沟通、战略对接、合作协调等方面持续发挥积极作用，引领次区域农业合作机制维护与建设。澜湄农业合作中心自成功设立后，发挥澜湄合作农业联合工作组的常设执行机构职责，履行区域性支持服务机构功能，推动澜湄农业合作中心国际化发展。积极落实《澜湄合作五年行动计划（2018—2022）》中"扩大农业科技领域的交流与合作，支持科研机构加强信息分享交流和人员互访"的建议，推动成立澜湄合作农业科技交流协作组，完善合作平台机制，为种植、畜牧和渔业领域的科技交流合作打下重要基础。推动设立澜湄农业合作广西分中心，依托广西—东盟农业合作的区位优势，助力澜湄农业科技、经贸和人才交流合作。澜湄农业合作产业协作组、澜湄动物兽药疫苗产业联盟、澜湄农业合作信息交流小组等合作小组有序筹备，逐步形成多合作小组、协作组、平台合作支撑体系，发挥技术支持、多方协调与信息沟通作用。

（二）稳步推进澜湄合作规划研究，促进知识分享与信息交流

起草《澜湄农业合作三年行动计划（2020—2022）》，该计划于澜湄合作第五次外长会期间正式通过，并列入澜湄合作第三次领导人会议成果。计划依托澜湄农业合作中心的协调支撑作用，聚焦农业合作政策对话、产业振兴、贸易发展等优先合作领域，在澜湄农业合作战略对接和项目实施中发挥指导作用。跟踪总结次区域澜湄农业合作进展、成效与经验，组织编制并正式出版《澜湄农业合作发展报告》，为澜湄合作农业联合工作组、各国有关部门与科研机构提供务实参考，促进农业合作全方位提质升级。开展地方省区农业基础调研，与科研机构、项目实施单位及企业加强合作，助力稻米、热带经济作物等重点产业的创新发展，推动农产品质量安全合作继续深化，提升次区域农业综合竞争力。

（三）协助统筹谋划澜湄农业项目，促进农业合作提质增效

项目聚焦种植业、畜牧、渔业等优势农业产业，协助亚洲合作资金申报实施，推动平台建设、联合研究、试验示范、能力建设等多个方面合作，促进澜湄次区域农业产业链、价值链优化升级。着力落实李克强总理在澜湄合作第三次领导人会议上的倡议，推动实施好"丰收澜湄"项目集群，从政策对话、产业发展、投资贸易、能力建设等方面，结合各国农业发展特点，聚焦重点领域和产业，推动实施一批优质项目，为建设澜湄流域经济发展带贡献重要力量。

四、项目影响

（一）推动澜湄农业合作机制日益完善

澜湄合作农业联合工作组高效运行，澜湄农业合作中心作为澜湄合作机制下设立的第四个中心，日益发挥区域性支持服务机构作用。

（二）推动农业农村政策沟通、经验交流与经贸对接平台逐步形成

通过举办澜湄农业农村发展合作论坛、推进"智农澜湄"平台模式化运营，不断强化多方协作与交流。

（三）聚焦重点产业，推动项目对接合作

通过协助开展澜湄农业合作项目统筹管理，聚焦重点产业领域，推动项目对接合作，助力区域重点产业发展与合作层次提升。

五、面临的困难与挑战

受新冠肺炎疫情影响，澜湄农业合作体系机制建设与联络交流工作受到一定影响。人员跨境流动受阻，活动难以正常开展，项目执行进度相对缓慢。"智农澜湄"平台在湄公河国家的推广应用受到影响。

六、成功经验

（一）创新形式，加强机制体系建设与维护工作

利用澜湄农业合作广西分中心、澜湄合作农业科技交流协作组等已有平台，发挥地方优势，与"走出去"企业、湄公河国家有关机构等保持交流联系，共同推动工作开展。

（二）整合资源，推进重点项目实施与品牌创建

整合项目资源，完善项目库建设。深入了解与挖掘各国农产品市场诉求，聚焦重点领域，推动实施好项目，争取湄公河各国支持，推动"丰收澜湄"项目集群有序开展，围绕重点项目，提出项目清单，完善项目库、专家库，树立项目品牌。

（三）加强宣传，做好澜湄农业合作基础信息收集与研究

加强宣传力度，定期梳理澜湄农业合作工作进展、研究成果、重点项目成效，通过媒体平台、会议论坛等多种渠道宣传推广。做好湄公河国家国别、重点产业信息收集和研究，提升技术支撑和政策建议能力，为机制体系完善提升、项目品牌实施打好基础。

案例二　以电视节目为媒介的澜湄区域全方位农业合作项目

一、项目目标

媒体是增进了解的窗口，深化友谊的纽带，促进合作的桥梁。澜湄合作机制确立了政治安全、经济可持续发展、社会人文三大支柱，媒体合作成为社会人文合作的重要组成部分。

以电视节目为媒介的澜湄区域全方位农业合作项目，旨在通过加强澜湄国家之间的媒体合作，加大对澜湄务实合作的传播力度，增进相互间的理解与信任，深化、创新澜湄六国媒体交流合作方式，搭建民心相通的纽带桥梁，厚植澜湄合作的民意基础，为推动构建澜湄国家命运共同体贡献力量。

二、项目活动

为响应澜湄合作倡议，推动澜湄农业合作不断向前发展，中国农业电影电视中心成功申报澜沧江—湄公河合作专项基金，于2019年10月共改编制作电视节目《中国农场》60期，主要涵盖科技类和致富经验类等内容，丰富了澜湄各国之间的农业和农村文化交流。

项目组派出多个摄制组，奔赴湄公河国家，拍摄制作《中国农场》新节目32期，其中科技类节目17期，讲述适合湄公河国家农业特点的种植养殖技术、产业发展经验和先进理念，拍摄选题包含椰子、木薯、草地贪夜蛾、火龙果、咖啡、可可、沉香、甘蔗、橡胶、胡椒、食用菌、哈密瓜等，如《木薯开发大有可为》《共同抗击草地贪夜蛾》等；双边合作类节目13期，介绍中国企业家联手湄公河国家农民创业的故事，以及澜湄国家互学互鉴与民心相通等内容，如《联手养出美味来》《只身在越南创业的中国人》《走向纵深的中泰农业合作》等；携手抗击贫困类节目2期，展现中国政府到湄公河流域国家开展扶贫工作的内容，如《中缅协作抗贫困》《中柬一家亲》。节目通过呈现人物内心情感、事业发展和人文关怀的相融相通，歌颂了澜湄六国间的深厚友谊。改编和新拍节目除在农视网等国内新媒体平台投放，还在湄公河国家主流媒体播出，以实现澜湄区域全媒体矩阵传播。

三、取得的成效

（一）增强了农业农村文化传播

《中国农场》是在湄公河国家播出的首个分享中国农业科技与致富经验的常态化专题电视节目。节目通过讲述农业故事、传播农人智慧，不仅让湄公河国家的城市观众关注农业、了解农业，更直接连通当地农民观众，与之分享切实可行的务农技术，推进湄公河国家间的文化沟通、农业联通、民心相通，进一步深化了澜湄六国间的合作与友谊。

（二）促进了农业技术交流分享

农业在澜湄国家经济发展中均占有重要地位。湄公河国家土壤肥沃、气候条件优异、农业人口众多，有着得天独厚的农业发展条件，利用先进科技快速发展农业需求迫切。湄公河国家版《中国农场》电视节目秉持农业节目始终追求的专业性、服务性、实用性，以媒为介，通过在湄公河国家主流媒体全年的常态化周播，将中国先进的农业种植养殖技术与致富经验和理念实实在在地分享给当地农民，逐渐帮助当地农民提高生产技能、平均产出与耕种效率，从而实现丰产丰收、脱贫致富、提升生活质量。

（三）加深了媒体间的沟通与交往

澜湄合作机制自启动以来展现出勃勃生机与活力，成为打造亚洲命运共同体的"金字招牌"。电视节目《中国农场》作为中国农业对外交流的一张名片，与湄公河国家主流媒体共同弘扬睦邻友好主旋律、宣介合作共赢新成果，合力营造支持促进澜湄合作的积极舆论氛围，为澜湄合作行稳致远、可持续发展保驾护航发挥了不可替代的重要作用。

四、项目影响

以《中国农场》为主的电视节目，深入实地，深耕合作对象国，通过建立有效的传播系统，与其他各国分享经验、知识和信息，为澜湄流域人民创造更多的福利，切实增进澜湄国家主流媒体间的合作和友谊，有效整合资源，形成一定的区域示范效应，强化可持续传播力。通过当地主流电视媒体进入当地家庭，普惠广大群众；使用当地官方语言播出，实现入耳入心入脑的有效传播，切实提高媒体知名度，建立媒体公信力。除了具备一定的文化交流效用，更重要的是了解澜湄农业合作所孕育的科技发展成果，通过学习相关知识，实现"看"以致用。

五、面临的困难与挑战

（一）节目播出的收视数据不明晰

由于大部分湄公河国家缺乏专业分析电视收视率、收视份额的市场研究公司，不具备对节目市场表现的洞察能力，导致《中国农场》电视节目在播出后面临无法收到直观数字反馈的问题，栏目的播出情况和满意度反馈主要来源于当地电视台和使馆。收视数据不明晰，将不利于节目优化提升。

（二）节目播出的期数不稳定

根据前期调查与了解，湄公河国家主流媒体对《中国农场》电视节目的排播情况存在多种不可控因素，如节假日将会取消节目排播等，将限制节目的播出期数。

六、成功经验

（一）严控节目制作的各个环节

根据项目执行实际情况，节目整体的片头、片花、主持人的选定和服饰以及演播室布景等多种要素，都与节目主题充分匹配，凸显了湄公河国家风情，使节目更合湄公河国家观众的胃口，从而达到节目实用性的最终效果。

（二）准确把握节目选题

节目选题不仅要符合湄公河国家农业特点和需求，还要对照时下最受湄公河国家关注的农业热点话题进行筛选，比如草地贪夜蛾的选题是2019年亚洲多国均面临且密切关注的农业安全问题。

（三）严格把控影视节目质量关

在内部严格审片、把控质量之后，为更好地把握政治尺度，保证节目内容与制作水平符合对外传播的质量标准与相关政策，项目邀请了多位专家对全部节目进行审看，制作组根据专家意见做出内容修改和提升，最终完成全部《中国农场》电视节目的制作。

（四）专业化译制

项目合作伙伴云南广播电视台国际频道依托自身独特的地缘优势，多年来聚集了一批东南亚、南亚小语种编译人才，并拥有以湄公河各国国家电视台播音员为主的译制人员力量，为《中国农场》电视节目的译制工作打下坚实基础。

（五）多平台播出

为扩大项目在澜湄国家的全面影响力，已制作好的《中国农场》中文版电视节目在农视网等国内新媒体平台播出；译制节目分别投放在中国农业电影电视中心的合作伙伴老挝国家电视台、柬埔寨商业电视台、缅甸Skynet 电视台、澜湄卫视等湄公河国家主流媒体播出。

第二篇 | 产业发展提升类

案例三　缅甸咖啡产量与质量提升项目

缅甸地处热带，气候温暖多雨、土壤肥沃，是优良的咖啡种植区，咖啡产业是缅甸农业最具发展潜力的领域之一。为实现与全球市场的有效对接，缅甸政府鼓励扩大咖啡种植面积，但是在种植技巧、加工技术以及机器设备等方面依然存在诸多不足，导致咖啡产量与质量提升严重受阻，亟待项目资金支持。在此背景下，以澜湄合作专项基金为依托，缅甸农业、畜牧与灌溉部实施了咖啡产量与质量提升项目。

一、项目目标

围绕咖啡产量与质量"双升"计划，项目目标主要集中在四个方面：一是探索创新性的咖啡种植技术，提升缅甸农民种植技能，提高缅甸咖啡产量；二是依托咖啡产业，提高缅甸农民收入，改善生活质量；三是改良咖啡品质，提高缅甸咖啡产品出口竞争力，形成国际贸易竞争优势；四是提高缅甸农民的管理技能，推动其从生产者转变为经营者，增强咖啡综合生产能力。

二、项目活动

(一)开展咖啡种植与加工培训

依托咖啡产量与质量提升项目，在缅甸钦邦、克钦邦、掸邦、曼德勒省和马圭省进行了 14 次专业咖啡生产培训，累计培训学员 1 639 名。此外，在缅甸勃固省和曼德勒省开展了 2 次"培训培训者"（Trainings of Trainers，TOT），并顺利完成对 97 名咖啡种植户的培训。

(二)组织考察学习

为学习咖啡种植与管护的前沿技术和成熟经验，2019 年 8 月 21—24 日，缅甸农业、畜牧与灌溉部派 6 名工作人员赴越南学习罗布斯塔咖啡的种植和加工技术。2020 年 6 月 29 日，组织缅甸钦邦的农民赴曼德勒省彬乌伦市考察咖啡研究信息推广与培训中心。2020 年 7 月 11 日，组织马圭省 Nat Yay Kan 村的农民赴咖啡技术发展农场考察，重点学习咖啡种植和加工技术。

（三）举办缅甸咖啡论坛

2019 年 5 月 15 日，在缅甸曼德勒省成功举办"缅甸咖啡论坛
（2019）"，共有 365 人出席（图 1）。此次论坛重点讨论了缅甸咖啡的
种植情况以及相关产业发展状况，探讨了咖啡生产和加工技术的国际
前沿问题，同时对当前阶段面临的困难与挑战进行了梳理总结。缅甸
咖啡论坛为发展咖啡产业汇聚了人脉，同时发挥了十分重要的宣传推
广作用。

图 1　缅甸咖啡论坛

（四）提供咖啡标准化生产服务

为实现标准化咖啡种植和质量管控，在项目执行期间，为项目区提供
了各类咖啡标准化生产服务，包括发放咖啡种子、种苗以及种植指南
（图 2）。其中，发放种子 109 千克、种苗 25.68 万株、遮阴树 2 万株。此
外，将现代化咖啡种植方法和技术编制成种植指南，发放给种植户，促进
其生产标准化和规范化。

（五）提供咖啡种植和加工基础设施

该项目提供的机器设备主要包括咖啡烘干托盘和制浆机两种，其中烘
干托盘 16 个（图 3）、制浆机 12 台。依托该项目，还向咖啡主产区提供了
螺旋传送带、折射仪、修剪剪刀、修剪锯和嫁接刀等实用工具。与此同
时，项目还购买了实验室设备，促进咖啡品质研究与质量提升，具体包括

图 2 咖啡种子和种植指南

实验室配套设备 1 套、制浆机 1 台、浆料机 1 台、烘焙机 1 台（图 4）以及质量评价实验室设备 1 套。

图 3 咖啡烘干托盘

图 4 咖啡豆烘焙机

三、取得的成效

（一）缅甸咖啡生产技术显著提高

通过举办咖啡生产培训班，对选种育苗、催芽定植、田间管理以及采收加工等过程进行专业培训，使缅甸农民掌握了科学的种植与加工技术，咖啡生产逐步趋向标准化和规范化。此外，在出国或跨区域考察学习过程中，农民的眼界不断开阔，学习和接受新生产技术的意愿和积极性不断增强。在此过程中，咖啡生产技术不断向前发展，技术水平日益提高，咖啡种植农户之间的交流学习产生了极大的溢出效应，扩大了生产技术的推广和普及范围，使得更多的群体受益于培训活动。

（二）缅甸咖啡产量和质量明显提升

在生产培训和对外交流学习过程中，缅甸咖啡的种植、加工逐步实现标准化，单产显著提高，总产量稳步上升。此外，通过烘干托盘、制浆机、烘焙机等机器设备的供应和使用，咖啡产品的制作工艺更加精良，品质明显改善，顺利实现与国际水平的接轨，国际贸易竞争力日益增强。

（三）缅甸农民收入与生活质量明显改善

咖啡产量与质量提升项目获得缅甸政府财政支持。其中，2018—2019财年，该项目获得的财政预算为11.7万美元；2019—2020财年，获得财政预算6.4万美元。在政府财政大力支持下，咖啡产业得到迅猛发展，产量与质量均有明显提升，特别是优质咖啡产量快速增长，实现了与国际市场的接轨，形成了明显的价格优势。在咖啡产量与价格两方面正向作用下，缅甸咖啡种植户的收入显著提高，生活质量得到明显改善。

四、项目影响

（一）项目成果显著

项目的预期目标是，在缅甸三地实施"双升"计划，开展专业咖啡生产培训4次，培训人数约250人，同时举办"培训培训者"活动1次。但实际执行远远超出预期，项目成果十分显著。其中，项目实施地扩大到6个，组织专业咖啡生产培训14次，累计培训学员达到1 639名，举办"培训培训者"（TOT）2次，培训人数97名。该项目得到切实执行，项目落地区域的农户可以应用现代技术生产高质量和特色咖啡，经济成效丰硕。

（二）项目发展潜力巨大

依托澜湄合作专项基金，缅甸咖啡产量与质量提升项目顺利推进，并取得显著成效。从现有成果来看，共有1 600余名咖啡种植户参加培训，97名咖啡种植户参与了"培训培训者"（TOT）。在中国的支持下，缅甸逐步建立起了咖啡产业，在相关配套措施推动下咖啡产业日趋稳定，进而形成咖啡产业增长极，其发展潜力十分巨大。与此同时，该项目的顺利实施使得中缅双边合作不断深入，双边交流更加通畅。

五、面临的困难与挑战

（一）项目执行依然存在资金缺口

一方面，由于汇率不稳定，项目资金换汇时存在贬值问题；另一方面，资金供给的及时性略有不足，特别是在新冠肺炎疫情期间，项目预算未得到及时修正，导致资金供给出现缺口，项目执行受到一定影响。

（二）技术研发缺乏高素质人员参与

为提高咖啡品质，项目在执行过程中提供了大量咖啡实验器材用于咖啡质量研究。但从事咖啡质量实验研究的人员十分匮乏，大多数参与者并不熟悉实验室仪器的操作和应用，导致咖啡品质提升面临局限性。

六、成功经验

（一）瞄准优势产业，激发产业潜力

从海拔、温度、降水量、供水、土壤、坡向和坡度等角度来看，缅甸具有种植高品质咖啡的天然优势。但受限于缅甸的基础条件，咖啡产业没有得到很好的开发，潜在的产业优势尚未得到挖掘，经济发展缺乏支柱性产业带动。依托澜湄合作专项基金，中国向缅甸提供专项资金支持，用于发展咖啡产业。在外部资金的支持下，缅甸的咖啡产业呈现迅猛发展趋势，项目成效基本达到预期水平。

（二）锁定单一领域，提供配套设施

缅甸咖啡产量与质量提升项目主要是锁定了单一的咖啡产品领域，提供了优质种苗、生产培训、出国或跨区域考察学习、机械设备以及实验器械等产前和产中配套的设施和服务支持。由于采取了"集中力量、全面突破"的项目实施策略，缅甸咖啡产业实现了跨越式发展，咖啡产量与质量实现双提升，农民收入与生活品质得到明显改善。

案例四　缅甸农村发展与蔬菜种植技术提升项目

缅甸是蔬菜生产国，具有成为蔬菜出口大国的潜力。然而，蔬菜是典型的知识密集型作物，这意味着种植蔬菜需要专业性的知识和劳动投入，菜农在较短的生产周期内种植多种蔬菜，对专业知识、种植技术和市场信息等基本素质提出了较高要求。但是，缅甸项目实施地区的大多数农民缺乏蔬菜种植技术，蔬菜管护知识十分匮乏。此外，由于农业投入品价格趋高，蔬菜种植成本一直处于高位，种植蔬菜收益有限。因此，为培植缅甸的蔬菜产业，拓展新的经济增长空间，需要为菜农提供蔬菜种植基本知识和信息，并且尝试将其用于指导实践。在此背景下，依托澜湄合作专项基金，缅甸农业、畜牧与灌溉部实施了农村发展与蔬菜种植技术提升项目。

一、项目目标

该项目以蔬菜产业为核心抓手，其目标主要有以下五个方面：一是借助缅甸蔬菜种植产业盘活农业生产力，提高农民经济收入和生活质量；二是通过蔬菜种植知识、技术和经验的学习和交流，增强缅甸蔬菜生产者及其加工群体的业务素质，提高其与现代农业的匹配性；三是培养一批蔬菜栽培技术人员，加强技术性人才对缅甸农业的支撑；四是实施蔬菜产业培训计划，建立农业技术培训长效机制，组建缅甸农民专家团队，提高对蔬菜栽培技术的科学认识；五是建立缅甸蔬菜示范农场，并将其作为社区教育中心，展示和宣传农业新理念和新技术。

二、项目活动

（一）开展基线数据调查

项目实施初期，选定 10 个主要的蔬菜种植区进行基线数据调查（图 1）。此项调查共询问了 200 余名农民，基于调查数据分析当前阶段蔬菜栽培技术的优势和劣势，并重点对存在的问题进行了提炼和总结。根据基线调查结果，以满足蔬菜种植户的实际需求为导向，项目组专家为其量身定制了蔬菜栽培技术体系和培训计划,切实解决菜农所需,提高了项目实施的针对性和有效性。

图 1　基线数据调查

(二)组织栽培技术培训

缅甸蔬菜和水果研究与开发中心对农民进行了蔬菜种植管理培训,并且编写技术培训手册(图2)。首先对50余名具有丰富蔬菜生产经验的农民进行培训,尝试建立农民专家团队。其次,在仰光省、勃固省和伊洛瓦底省选定9个村庄进行农民培训,共有450余名蔬菜种植户参加了培训,培训周期为7天。培训内容主要有以下16项:蔬菜栽培指南、土壤养分管理、蔬菜种质培育、杂交种质培育、土壤肥力评价(理论+实践)、天然肥料和农药制作(理论+实践)、蚯蚓养殖和堆肥(理论+实践)、有机农业(理论+实践)、GAP蔬菜生产(理论+实践)、蔬菜采后管理、全年蔬菜生产、应对气候变化的蔬菜反季生产、家庭园艺、病虫害防控、防护栽培技术以及蔬菜种子管理与贮藏技术。

图 2　栽培技术培训

（三）建立示范农场并开展农民田间日活动

项目组选择在仰光省、勃固省和伊洛瓦底省建立示范农场，并且将其作为农业教育中心开展农民田间日活动（图3）。以示范农场为资助重点，该项目向试点农户提供种子、化肥、农药、喷雾器以及修剪工具等投入品，从产前和产中提供蔬菜技术支持。与此同时，还为示范农场指定蔬菜专家团队，指导不同种类的蔬菜种植，形成示范标准后，邀请相关地区的农民和观察员前来学习蔬菜栽培技术。

图 3 示范农场与农民田间日活动

（四）开展与澜湄国家的技术交流

项目组赴越南开展为期7天的蔬菜栽培技术交流活动。此次交流活动共有10位专家参加，主要考察了河内蔬菜研究所，以及河内、达南、哈龙等地区主要蔬菜生产基地。此外，项目组还对越南南部农业科学研究所、和知县马铃薯研究中心和越南南部的蔬菜种植区进行了深入调研，重点对蔬菜的市场信息、栽培技术（水培和气培系统）以及食品安全等问题进行了详细考察。

三、取得的成效

根据预期目标，项目得到了切实执行，并且取得了丰硕成效，具体表现为以下四个方面。

（一）基线数据调查成果丰硕

项目实施初期，项目组首先收集了 10 个项目实施地区土壤和水资源样本，对其营养成分、有机质含量、矿物质含量、生物学指标进行了检测，进而对调查地区是否适合蔬菜种植进行了科学评估，形成了系统的评估报告。

（二）蔬菜示范农场初具规模

依托该项目，已经在 10 个地区建立了示范农场，举办农民田间日活动多期，形成了强大的辐射带动作用，使大批蔬菜种植户受益。

（三）蔬菜栽培培训成果显著

该项目已在 4 个地区开展蔬菜栽培培训讲习班，累计培训 240 余人。与此同时，共计 10 人前往越南参与蔬菜栽培技术交流，根据考察资料形成研究报告和视频报告（图 4）。

图 4　澜湄国家蔬菜栽培技术交流

（四）蔬菜种植收益增长明显

项目实施期间，蔬菜种植户的收益明显增长。调查数据发现，2019—2020 年，平均 1 英亩①蔬菜现金净收益增长 7.2％～21.2％，其中种植茄子的收益增长率最高（21.2％）（表 1）。

总体上项目成效显著，蔬菜产业呈现跨越式发展趋势。

---

① 英亩为我国非法定计量单位，1 英亩＝4 046.856 米²。下同。——编者注

表 1　2019—2020 年蔬菜亩均净收益以及增长率

单位：缅甸元/英亩，%

蔬菜作物	2019 年净收益	2020 年净收益	增长率
茄子	540 000	654 480	21.2
长豆	350 000	396 900	13.4
秋葵	565 000	662 745	17.3
萝卜	230 000	246 560	7.2
绿辣椒	265 000	316 675	19.5
甜玉米	375 000	408 000	8.8
平均水平	387 500	447 560	15.5

四、项目影响

(一)缅甸绿色农业得到有效推进

项目执行过程中缅甸菜农心态与技术发生了明显变化，表现为对蔬菜种植的信心增强，知识和技术水平显著提高。特别是在参加项目培训后，缅甸菜农对有机农业技术在蔬菜领域的应用产生了浓厚兴趣。具体而言，菜农能够熟练制作生物肥料和有机投入要素，例如利用蚯蚓堆肥、天然叶面肥料、发酵果汁以及鱼氨基酸等作为有机肥料。通过该项目，大多数农民对绿色农业有了深刻认识，人们开始重视农业的可持续性，并且能够在实际行动中减少农药、化肥等化学品的投入，使绿色农业得到切实发展。

(二)项目满意度极高

2020 年 9 月，对项目实施情况进行了满意度评价分析。首先，从项目实施地仰光省、勃固省和伊洛瓦底省分别选取 12 名经过培训的菜农，然后对其进行问卷调查。数据显示，缅甸菜农对该项目实施表现出较高满意度。其中，16% 菜农的满意度评分为 100 分，40% 评分为 80 分，43% 评分为 60 分，没有人对项目实施表示不满意。项目实施基本达到了预期目标，使参与者能够从中获益，并且极大促进了地区经济发展，赢得了缅甸菜农高度认可。

（三）中缅合作进一步加深

缅甸农村发展与蔬菜种植技术提升项目是澜湄合作专项基金的项目之一。通过该项目实施，中缅双方都能够在合作中汲取发展成果，认识到了双边合作的重要性。以该项目为依托，中缅双方将开展更广领域更深层次的交流合作，积极创造帮扶对接机会，推动区域经济一体化。

五、面临的困难与挑战

（一）菜农的培训效率偏低

项目地区大多数农民主要遵循传统种植技术，利用新技术和新方法从事蔬菜种植的观念或意识不强，导致相关技术培训效率比较低，短期成效不显著。此外，项目地区农户文化水平普遍偏低，对于新技术、新观念、新方法的认知度不足，对蔬菜栽培技术培训和各类讲习班所传递的理论知识难以接受、知识消化更为困难，难以发挥对实践的指导作用。

（二）辐射带动作用尚未显现

当前，受益群体集中为项目参与者。从已经取得的成效来看，项目执行过程中参与者数量仍然较少，项目落地实施的区域存在局限性，同时项目也未得到较好宣传。上述种种原因导致该项目惠及的群体面较小，其潜在的溢出效应和辐射带动作用没有得到切实挖掘和有效发挥。

六、成功经验

（一）开展基线调查，做到有的放矢

在项目实施初期，对项目实施区的土壤和水资源进行了营养成分、有机质含量、矿物质含量、生物学指标检测，并且对蔬菜种植的适应性进行了科学评估，这为后期项目顺利开展奠定了重要基础。事实上，农业的强弱主要受资源禀赋的影响，其优势和潜力往往取决于气候、土壤和水资源状况。因此，在实施农业项目之前进行必要的资源条件检测必不可少，这样可以实现有的放矢，规避不必要的损失。

（二）建立示范农场，打造成功样板

在项目执行过程中，在仰光省、勃固省和伊洛瓦底省建立蔬菜示范农场，并且以蔬菜示范农场为资助重点，对其提供种子、化肥、农药、喷雾

器以及修剪工具等投入品，推动示范农场发展。一方面，蔬菜示范农场是典型的成功样板，具有很强的示范带动作用，可以为其他农场提供发展指南。另一方面，蔬菜示范农场具有"由点及面""先强带动后强"的作用，通过集中有限的资金、人才、技术为示范农场提供支持，发挥集中力量办大事的作用；发展成熟的农场则可以进一步带动其他农场发展，同时还可以发挥后发优势，提高整体发展速度。

（三）紧抓事后反馈，适时调整策略

项目执行成效需要进行科学的事后调查评估。项目实施后期对仰光省、勃固省和伊洛瓦底省的参与者进行了满意度调查，并且系统分析了反馈信息。这样可以更好地把握项目实施的真实效果，包括是否能够惠及农民、是否可以带动农村经济发展、是否实现了预期目标等。与此同时，在客观评估项目成效基础上，针对可能存在的短板可以适时调整实施策略，及时修正不足之处。

案例五 澜湄次区域水稻绿色增产技术试验示范项目

澜湄次区域水稻绿色增产技术试验示范项目是澜湄农业合作在种植业方面的重点项目，该项目由广西农业职业技术学院联合多家跨国农业企业，在柬埔寨、缅甸、老挝、越南四个国家开展水稻绿色增产技术试验示范和稻田综合种养模式试验，旨在提高澜湄次区域水稻绿色增产技术应用水平，促进各区域水稻产业绿色、高质、高效发展。

一、项目目标

项目基于广西与东盟国家气候相似、地域相近等区域优势，以及广西形成的适用于低纬度地区的水稻绿色增产技术和模式，分别在柬埔寨、缅甸、老挝、越南建成农作物优良品种试验站，以此为技术交流推广平台，示范推广适合各区域的水稻绿色增产技术和模式。通过项目的实施，一方面有利于推进澜湄各区域粮食生产实现绿色、高产、高质、高效并重的目标，确保区域粮食安全；另一方面，通过对澜湄各区域农民生产技术培训与技术帮扶，促进当地农民增收和农业可持续发展。

二、项目活动

项目开展了水稻新品种引进与示范、水稻绿色增产技术改良、稻田综合种养模式试验、人员培训与展示推介以及优化组装适合当地的水稻绿色增产技术等活动。具体如下：

（一）建立水稻绿色增产技术试验示范基地

通过建立水稻绿色增产技术试验示范基地，围绕主推品种开展播种、育秧、水肥管理和病虫害防控等技术试验示范（图1）。截至2020年底，项目共建立试验示范基地8 655亩，辐射带动面积超过44 030亩。其中柬埔寨4 710亩，辐射带动14 000亩；缅甸1 560亩，辐射带动10 030亩；老挝820亩，辐射带动8 000亩；越南1 565亩，辐射带动超过12 000亩。

图1　缅甸进行的水稻绿色增产技术试验示范项目

（二）开展水稻新品种引进和示范

从中国引进一批品质优、产量高、抗性好、适应性强的水稻新品种到项目所在国进行试验和筛选（图2）。截至2020年底，共从中国引进水稻品种44个，筛选出适合当地的优良品种15个。其中柬埔寨引进25个，筛选出9个；缅甸引进5个，筛选出1个；老挝引进11个，筛选出2个；越南引进3个，筛选出3个。同时将中国引进品种与当地品种进行对比试验。

图2　中国（广西）—老挝农作物优良品种试验站水稻
绿色增产技术试验示范项目品种比较试验

（三）开展稻田综合种养模式试验

围绕发展稻虾、稻渔、稻鸭等稻田综合种养模式，在柬埔寨开展绿色水稻种植相应的综合种养技术试验示范和推广（图3）。项目共引入6个试验品种分别进行稻虾、稻渔、稻鸭等稻田综合种养试验示范，经测算，稻鸭模式投入成本和风险最小，但收益较低，每亩增加经济收益 220 元人民币；稻渔模式需要进行稻田改造，投入成本和风险最高，但收益也高，每亩增加经济收益 413 元人民币。项目计划在柬埔寨改造虾田 212 英亩，实施稻田套养罗氏沼虾项目，预计每亩增加经济收益 3 000 元人民币。

图 3　柬埔寨开展的稻田套养罗氏沼虾项目

（四）开展人员培训与展示推介活动

依托中国（广西）—东盟农作物优良品种试验站和广西境外农业合作示范区平台以及项目所在国农业合作单位的推广体系，开展水稻高产、优质、高效栽培技术及病虫害防控技术、农业机械使用及维修等方面的培训。截至目前，共开展技术培训 50 多期，培训当地农户和技术人员 1 496人次。中国（广西）—老挝农作物优良品种试验站在老挝举办了一次现场指导和成果展示推介活动，共有 12 户种植户参加。

（五）优化组装适合当地的水稻绿色增产技术

根据当地实际情况，优化组装了适合当地的水稻绿色增产技术。如在柬埔寨优化了水稻机械穴直播新技术；在老挝组装推广了集中育秧、机插秧、水气平衡、"三控"栽培、精准施肥、稻草还田、重大病虫害综合治理等技术，建立标准化水稻生产种植技术标准，并编写适合当地的水稻绿色增产技术规程 1 套；在缅甸优化了集中育苗培育壮秧、直播、抛秧等方式，促进施用有机肥、农家肥，并推动田间投入使用振频式杀虫灯和黄板；在越南开展了水稻直播栽培试验示范（图 4）。

图4 越南开展的水稻绿色增产技术试验示范项目

三、取得的成效

(一)澜湄次区域水稻绿色增产技术应用水平不断提高

澜湄次区域水稻绿色增产技术试验示范基地的建设推广,提高了柬埔寨、缅甸、老挝、越南四国水稻绿色增产技术应用水平。总体来看,项目共建立试验示范基地 8 655 亩,辐射带动面积超过 44 030 亩,平均每亩试验示范基地带动当地 5 亩以上稻田应用水稻绿色增产技术;从各区域来看,柬埔寨、缅甸、老挝、越南平均每亩试验示范基地分别带动当地约 3.0 亩、6.4 亩、9.8 亩、7.7 亩稻田应用水稻绿色增产技术。

(二)澜湄次区域水稻生产增产增效显著

新品种的引进示范、水肥管理、病虫害防控等技术的推广应用,均有效推动了澜湄次区域水稻生产增产增效。一方面,品质优、产量高、抗性好、适应性强的水稻新品种的引进、试验和筛选为澜湄次区域水稻提质增产提供了种质保障,项目区共从中国引进水稻品种 44 个,筛选出适合当地的优良品种达 15 个;另一方面水稻绿色增产技术的推广应用,不仅大幅减少了化肥、农药用量,提高了水稻绿色生产水平,还降低了病虫害造成的损失及防治成本,并提高了水稻产量及品质,增强了该区域水稻的市场竞争力。例如,柬埔寨采用的水稻机械穴直播新技术,在有效减少病虫害的同时,每亩水稻增产 25.9%,增收节支达

159.5 元；老挝、缅甸、越南通过优化组装适合当地的水稻绿色增产技术，每亩水稻分别增产 47.4％、10.2％和 10.3％，增收分别达 120 元、210 元和 112 元。

（三）澜湄次区域农民与技术人员技能得到提升

通过开展水稻高产、优质、高效栽培技术及病虫害防控技术、农业机械使用及维修等方面的培训，提升了该区域农民与技术人员技能。对于农户，技术培训与示范推广转变了其在病虫害防控上的传统观念，通过比较应用效果，农民切实认识到了该技术的作用；对于技术人员，50 多期的技术培训大幅提高了其水稻绿色增产相关技术的应用水平。

四、项目影响

（一）开展境外试验示范，打造产业合作关键支撑

澜湄次区域水稻绿色增产技术试验示范项目作为农业对外合作的重要手段之一，在深化国际交流合作中发挥了重要作用。根据当地实际情况引入中国较为成熟的育秧、栽培、水肥管理和病虫害绿色防控等技术，开展绿色水稻综合种养技术试验示范和推广，在保护当地生态环境的前提下实现了增产增收，为推动当地水稻提质增效提供了有效技术支撑，也为水稻科研育种提供了科学依据。

（二）突出联络驻外涉农部门，增强外事服务能力

项目实施过程中，务实地为当地水稻生产提供诸多公益性服务，切实提高当地农业生产技术水平，促进农业增产增收，对服务国家外交大局发挥了积极作用，得到了项目所在国农业部门的高度赞赏。同时，基地发挥根植当地基层、有当地朋友圈的优势，促进国内农业生产管理和科技人员通过基地深入了解所在国农业、农村、农民实际，为更好促进农业交流合作提供决策依据。

五、面临的困难与挑战

（一）政策制约，种苗引进受阻

项目推进过程中适逢柬埔寨大选，柬埔寨农林渔业部暂停虾苗引进的

审批工作，按正常流程引进虾苗并进行稻虾综合种养试验示范受阻，影响项目实施过程中的部分工作进度。同时，中国与柬埔寨就水产品进出口检验检疫尚未达成协议，也直接导致了项目不能按时按计划从中国广西壮族自治区水产科学研究院引进罗氏沼虾虾苗，而改从柬埔寨水产科学院引苗，无法实现稻虾养成上市的目标。

（二）品种不适且配套设施薄弱，项目实施难度大

项目从中国引进的克氏原螯虾进入柬埔寨后，由于光温、气候、水文条件的不同，加上柬埔寨当地无石灰进行塘底消毒，小龙虾出现肠炎、脱壳不遂以及白斑综合征等病状，根据专家意见必须进行虾沟改造后再开展第二次综合稻虾种养试验。受客观条件影响，项目国普遍存在基础设施建设不够完善、农资供应相对缺乏、自然灾害预警滞后等问题，增加了项目实施的难度。

（三）农民观念落后，新技术接受意愿偏弱

当地老百姓受传统观念影响，种植水稻自给自足，很少有将水稻作为商品的概念，"看天吃饭"的观念普遍存在，对新品种新技术的接受需要一个过程。且当前新技术主要以试验示范为应用及推广途径，示范基地的辐射范围仍有限，不能全面辐射到当地农民，仍需要一定的时间来推广技术。

六、成功经验

（一）政府重视，科学合理规划

政府重视是水稻绿色增产技术得以顺利推广的重要保障。澜湄各国高度重视水稻绿色增产技术试验示范项目，由各承担单位联合当地的农业部门成立专门项目领导小组，研究制定项目实施方案，通过定期汇报、跟踪执行、实地检查等方式，及时了解项目执行情况和存在的问题，并协调解决。

（二）落实责任，强化考核措施

加强对项目工作检查督导，要求各项目承担单位对照任务合同书，逐项落实工作目标任务，量化考核指标，制定全年具体实施方案，保证项目工作顺利完成。相关政府部门强化对水稻绿色增产技术的重视，增加水稻

绿色增产技术的覆盖范围，实行跟踪式指导，保证农户具备一定的专业知识，能够应对水稻种植期间的各类问题，切实保障水稻绿色栽培增产增效。

（三）建设基地，促进技术推广

新技术的推广和应用需要一定的过程，而技术的试验示范是促进技术推广和应用的重要手段之一。该项目通过建设水稻绿色增产技术试验示范基地，辐射带动了周边种植户应用新的生产技术。基地辐射带动的效果相对较好，平均每亩试验示范基地带动了 5 亩以上稻田应用新技术，为技术的推广和应用奠定了重要基础。

（四）因地制宜，推广适宜技术

不同地区因地理位置、自然禀赋、气候条件等多方面因素存在差异，水稻生产情况存在不同特征，而且各地区经济发展水平、技术应用水平也存在一定差异。该项目结合各地区特征，在不同地区进行了适应地区特征的技术试验示范，这也为技术推广和应用奠定了坚实的基础，同时也较好满足了当地水稻绿色生产技术的需求。

案例六　澜湄橡胶树栽培技术及加工示范基地建设项目

天然橡胶与钢铁、石油和煤炭并列为四大工业原料，是其中唯一的可再生资源，是重要的战略物资之一。然而，橡胶树种植受地理环境条件的制约较大。澜湄流域大部分地区地处热带、高湿、无风地区，拥有天然的地理条件，是橡胶树的传统种植区域。澜湄橡胶树栽培技术及加工示范基地建设项目通过详尽调研澜湄天然橡胶产业发展中存在的问题，针对橡胶树栽培、采收生产和胶乳加工等技术环节提升需求情况，提供橡胶树栽培及加工技术，并进行示范基地建设。项目的实施提升了当地橡胶产品品质，促进了澜湄国家橡胶产业的发展。

一、项目目标

针对澜湄天然橡胶产业存在栽培技术落后、病虫害发病率高、死皮发生率高、天然橡胶加工领域以传统烟片胶生产加工为主、没有技术分级橡胶的加工技术及平台等方面的问题，结合中国在抗旱栽培、高产栽培、死皮防控、割胶技术和天然生胶技术分级橡胶（凝胶级）加工领域创新性技术优势，中国热带农业科学院橡胶研究所联合柬埔寨橡胶研究所、越南橡胶研究所、泰国橡胶局、老挝云橡有限责任公司、缅甸农业、畜牧与灌溉部多年生作物司以及缅甸橡胶种植和生产商协会，在各国橡胶树核心产区选址并建成橡胶树高产高效综合栽培技术和抚管示范基地30～50亩，集成示范推广中国成熟的橡胶树割胶技术以及乙烯灵、死皮康、电动割胶刀和干胶测定仪自动化收胶系统等新型产品和设备，为推动澜湄国家橡胶树栽培和加工技术进步，进一步深化各国在橡胶树育种、栽培、割胶和加工等橡胶全产业链的合作提供重要平台。

二、项目活动

项目根据柬埔寨、老挝、缅甸、泰国和越南天然橡胶产业发展需求，将中国成熟的栽培和加工技术进行引入和示范推广，建设天然橡胶割胶技术示范基地，输入先进的产品与设备，并对设备选型与设备操作进行技术培训。

2018年6月27日—7月6日，项目科研人员赴老挝执行澜湄国际合作项目任务。开展澜湄区域橡胶林植物多样性研究，同时对老挝橡胶园的管理模式、割胶制度及产量、橡胶林及典型热带作物的空间分布等进行指导。

2019年11月，澜湄合作成果展在老挝万象国际贸易会展中心举办。与会各国对澜湄国家的发展有了更多的了解和认识，为各方加强橡胶原料收购、橡胶产品销售、橡胶和农产品行业技术、橡胶和农产品检验检疫、橡胶技术培训等领域的交流与合作提供了更多可能性。

2020年上半年，中国与柬埔寨橡胶研究所、缅甸农业、畜牧与灌溉部多年生作物司、缅甸橡胶种植和生产商协会达成协议，分别在柬埔寨橡胶核心产区特本克蒙省和缅甸橡胶核心产区仰光省合作建设天然橡胶割胶技术示范基地50亩（图1）。根据示范基地示范技术的差异，分别向柬埔寨橡胶研究所运送基地建设所需橡胶树专用肥料、电动胶刀、微生物肥料、增产素和死皮康等物资104件；向缅甸橡胶种植和生产商协会运输肥料、增产素、电动胶刀和干胶测定仪72件。针对柬埔寨橡胶研究所对橡胶树有机肥料生产和叶部病害分离鉴定的需求，购买了橡胶树病理和生理

图1　柬埔寨中、英、柬三国语言基地示范牌

学检测分析仪器 5 台，用于技术培训；同时，为柬埔寨橡胶研究所烟片胶加工生产线改造，运送了五合一压片机、凝固槽和铝合金板等耗材，并提供技术指导。印刷《橡胶研究所死皮康技术示范手册》等技术示范手册10 种（表 1）。针对新冠肺炎疫情大流行带来的出访困难，项目开展了线上培训，培训各国科技人员和工人 200 人次以上，满意度为 100%，显著提升了示范基地的生产水平，基地生产和环境水平明显高于当地平均水平。

表 1   中国热带农业科学院橡胶研究所澜湄合作项目系列技术示范手册

序号	名称
1	橡胶研究所死皮康技术示范手册
2	橡胶研究所 4CJX－303B 电动胶刀技术示范手册
3	橡胶研究所增产素技术示范手册
4	橡胶研究所 4GXJ－2 电动胶刀示范手册
5	橡胶研究所干胶含量测定仪技术示范手册
6	橡胶研究所籽苗芽接技术示范手册
7	橡胶研究所高效栽培技术示范手册
8	橡胶研究所专用肥技术示范手册
9	橡胶树病害鉴定技术示范手册
10	橡胶树微生物肥料技术示范手册

2021 年，项目克服新冠肺炎疫情影响，通过开展线上技术指导和培训示范、制作技术操作视频和手册等方式，分别与柬埔寨橡胶研究所、云橡投资有限公司（老挝）签订电子合作协议，合作开展橡胶树栽培技术及加工示范基地建设及加工生产线改造等工作。

三、取得的成效

（一）栽培示范基地建设成效显著

项目分别与柬埔寨橡胶研究所，缅甸农业、畜牧与灌溉部多年生作物司以及缅甸橡胶种植和生产商协会合作，累计在柬埔寨和缅甸建设天然橡胶割胶技术示范基地 100 亩，显著提升了示范基地的生产水平，基地生产和环境水平明显高于当地平均水平，为推动橡胶树栽培技术示范推广提供了必要的基础条件。

（二）加工技术和生产线水平提高

项目为柬埔寨橡胶研究所烟片胶加工厂进行技术分级橡胶（凝胶级）加工示范生产线厂房选址、基建改造、设备选型、水电安装、运行调试等指导，提供了不锈钢凝固槽和铝合金板等耗材，显著提高生产效率，为初加工技术提升和生产线产能提升提供了技术支持（图 2）。

柬埔寨烟片胶加工厂旧凝固槽　　　　中国热带科学院橡胶研究所
　　　　　　　　　　　　　　　　　提供的新不锈钢凝固槽

图 2　柬埔寨烟片胶加工厂新旧凝固槽对比

（三）技术培训指导效果显著

通过线上、视频和技术手册等多种方式提供橡胶树栽培和加工技术培训，提高了澜湄五国橡胶生产加工水平，促进了橡胶树割胶技术以及乙烯灵、死皮康、电动割胶刀和干胶测定仪自动化收胶系统等新型产品和设备的示范推广，如死皮康水剂的增产效果比当地提高了 3.32 倍、土壤颗粒剂的增产效果提高了 2.76 倍，也提升了当地橡胶生产技术水平。

(四)澜湄橡胶产业发展水平有所提升

一方面，提升了当地橡胶产量和加工产品品质，促进了橡胶产品的销售和贸易，提升了经济效益和胶工收入；另一方面，通过举办澜湄合作成果展，让与会各国对澜湄国家橡胶产业有了更深入的认识与了解，为澜湄国家开展橡胶产品的贸易、合作、技术交流提供了渠道。

四、项目影响

项目在国际橡胶研究和发展委员会和天然橡胶生产国协会等国际组织平台框架内展开了深入的学术交流与合作，与东南亚相关国家开展了品种交换、技术培训和学术交流等工作。目前，已签订了《柬埔寨王国柬埔寨橡胶研究所和中华人民共和国中国热带农业科学院橡胶研究所橡胶研究合作协议》，具有良好的合作基础。

项目所提出的合作内容具有前瞻性和创新性，符合双方需求和优势，选择的合作方式和实施方案可行，任务和目标设定合理，有利于提高双方科学研究水平和综合创新能力，促进双方相关产业发展。项目对推动澜湄国家橡胶树栽培和加工技术进步，对接"一带一路"倡议，促进澜湄国际组织平台框架内展开全方位合作交流和后续深入的技术交流与合作，起到了显著的促进作用。

五、面临的困难与挑战

受新冠肺炎疫情影响，2020 年度项目执行遇到困难。主要是出国和邀请国外专家培训无法按计划进行，国际运输成本上涨，双方邮寄资料延滞。

为了保证项目的顺利执行，积极利用信息化手段，拓展境外伙伴关系，取得了一定成效。但技术交流与试验示范类项目境外活动进展有限，邀请国外技术人员来华培训也未成行。培训项目因设备操作复杂程度等因素，仅靠线上方式进行培训，给实现技术培训预期效果增加了难度。

六、成功经验

（一）精心组织和策划实施

项目执行单位积极组织项目策划实施，与澜湄国家橡胶研究机构沟通协商，签署协议、制定研究计划。示范基地建设所依据的原则是选择国家级部属单位进行合作，基地选址为天然橡胶主产区，选择当地主栽品种，所选林段林相整齐。同时，基地交通便利，科研人员和胶工管理专业。

（二）科学调研，使技术支持有的放矢

示范技术选择的原则是结合前期调研和所选基地建设基础，结合合作方的需求，制定不同示范技术和方案。示范基地建成后，通过持续跟踪指导合作基地建设和开展技术示范，如联合柬埔寨橡胶研究所，缅甸农业、畜牧与灌溉部多年生作物司以及缅甸橡胶种植和生产商协会专家协同调研两国天然橡胶资源分布、割胶制度、割胶技术等现状，并由合作方提出技术需求，使推动当地橡胶产业发展、进行技术推广示范更具有针对性和精准性。

（三）以技术指导加设备保障的方式助推橡胶生产技术提升

项目为柬埔寨橡胶研究所烟片胶加工生产线改造提供了技术指导，并提供了五合一压片机、不锈钢凝固槽和铝合金板等耗材，从技术和物资方面支持柬埔寨橡胶研究所烟片胶加工生产线改造。同时，考虑到当地缺少技术配套设施，中国热带科学院橡胶研究所提供配套设备保障，有效解决了这一问题，既保证了技术示范效果，又推动了后续加工工艺改造的技术效率提升。

案例七　澜湄水生生物保护及渔业合作项目

澜沧江—湄公河是亚洲最重要的跨国水系，连接澜湄六国，鱼类物种多样性位居世界第三。近年来，在气候干旱、水电等涉水工程开发、非法捕捞等影响下，澜湄流域生态环境日益恶化，水生生物资源受到不同程度的影响，湄公江豚面临灭绝风险，经济发展和生态保护之间的矛盾逐渐显现。如何在发展经济的同时保护水生生物多样性，促进资源可持续利用，是亟待解决的问题。澜湄水生生物保护及渔业合作项目由中国农业农村部长江流域渔政监督管理办公室组织实施，聚焦澜湄流域渔业和水生态养护交流合作机制建设、水产养殖技术培训、联合执法暨增殖放流、水生生物资源养护等重点工作，推动澜湄流域水生生物资源养护工作有效开展。

一、项目目标

项目旨在推动全方位、多领域的澜湄流域水生态保护合作，提升澜湄国家水生生物资源养护水平，切实推进澜湄流域渔业和水生态养护交流合作机制建设，深化中国与湄公河流域国家全方位友好合作。项目在总结前期澜湄合作成果的基础上，将重点在水生生物保护及渔业合作等方面开展务实合作，实现共建绿色澜湄的目标。通过实施水生生物保护及渔业合作项目，聚焦发展合作，研究澜湄流域绿色高质量发展路径，按照"发展为先、务实高效、项目为本"的模式，打造协同联动发展格局推进澜湄流域渔业和水生态合作"年年上台阶"。此外，发挥科研院所科技资源优势，开展澜湄流域国家渔业资源管理和水产养殖发展技术培训工作，提高澜湄国家渔业资源管理水平和当地土著鱼类养殖水平，减轻自然渔业资源利用压力，推动澜湄流域绿色经济发展带建设。

二、项目活动

项目实施单位自 2018 年开始持续有序开展澜湄水生生物保护及渔业合作项目相关工作，推进澜湄流域水生态交流合作机制建设，促进澜湄流域渔业和水生态合作走深走实。

（一）联合国际组织共同发起澜湄流域资源养护分论坛

2018 年 11 月，中国农业农村部举办了长江生物资源保护论坛—澜湄流域生物资源养护分论坛，分论坛主题为"发展可持续渔业，共建和谐澜湄"，旨在积极贯彻落实"一带一路"倡议和澜湄合作机制的重要部署（图 1）。近 70 位来自澜湄国家的领导、专家学者齐聚一堂，共同探讨保护生态资源，推动澜湄流域渔业可持续发展。在澜湄流域水生生物资源保护、澜湄长效合作机制的建立等方面达成了多项共识。论坛的成功举办，初步构建了"政府主导、企业配合、全民参与、国际支持"的工作格局。

图 1　澜湄流域生物资源养护分论坛参会人员合影

（二）和柬埔寨签订合作备忘录，达成合作共识

2017 年，中国农业农村部长江流域渔政监督管理办公室与柬埔寨农林渔业部渔业局签订《中国与柬埔寨澜沧江—湄公河水生生物资源养护合作备忘录》，将合作开展湄公河豚类就地迁地保护工作，开展渔业增殖放流及资源环境监测，建立信息互通机制和渔政联合执法，共同加强澜沧江—湄公河流域水生生物资源和水域生态环境保护工作。

（三）澜湄联合增殖放流工作取得重要进展

增殖放流是澜湄合作机制 45 项早期收获项目之一。2017 年，联合老挝、柬埔寨、泰国等国家的渔业行政主管部门共同开展增殖放流活动，增殖放流苗总计 219.3 万尾，完成率为 365.5%，超额完成了项目的增殖放流数量指标。2018 年 7 月，参加柬埔寨第 16 届国家放鱼日活动，并与柬埔寨农林渔业部就澜湄合作机制框架下水生生物保护合作进行交流（图2）。2018年，分别于5月在泰国、7月在柬埔寨、11月在云南省西双版纳开展澜湄流域增殖放流活动。2019年7月10日，联合老挝自然资源与环境部、南塔省自然资源与环境厅，中国云南省农业农村厅、西双版纳傣族自治州农业农村局及相关单位在云南西双版纳共同开展2019年中老联合执法暨增殖放流活动。2019年7月13—14日，参加2019年老挝南塔省"三八"河①增殖放流活动，并向老挝南塔省赠送增殖放流鱼苗23万尾，其中鲤鱼20万尾、丝尾鳠2万尾、大鳞四须鲃1万尾。本次增殖放流活动已经是中国第五年赴老挝南塔省参加水生野生动物保护日的"放鱼日"活动，五年间累计赠送增殖放流鱼苗61.4万尾，其中鲤鱼56万尾、丝尾鳠4.4万尾、大鳞四须鲃1万尾，极大保护和补充了流域内的水生生物资源（图3）。

图2 《中国与柬埔寨澜沧江—湄公河水生生物资源养护合作备忘录》签署现场

（四）开展湄公江豚种群科学考察

2019年，赴柬埔寨湄公河段开展两次湄公江豚科学考察（图4）。考察发现柬埔寨湄公河段湄公江豚主要分布在4～6米处深水区，累计估算该河段湄公江豚种群数量约为76～80头，加强了中柬两国在澜湄流域濒危物种保护及资源养护方面的合作与交流，保障了澜湄水生生物保护及渔

---

① "三八"河指位于老挝南塔河的一处由妇女负责的自然保护区。

业合作项目的顺利实施。

图 3　2019 年放流现场

图 4　湄公江豚种群考察团队合影

（五）中老两国渔政执法合作不断深化

2015 年 11 月，中国与老挝开展了首次澜湄渔政联合执法行动，开创了两国渔政联合执法新模式，开启了两国共同管理和养护澜湄水生生物资源和水域生态环境的新篇章，建立了长效合作机制。2017 年 12 月，中国和老挝共同开展"2017 中国·老挝澜湄渔政联合执法行动暨增殖放流活动"。双方不断加强沟通、凝聚共识、深化合作，共同致力澜湄水生生物资源和水域生态环境保护，并建立了定期互访机制。2018 年集中销毁在边境水域收缴的电鱼具（器）、网具近百顶（套），放流当地鱼苗 7 万尾。2019 年 7 月，中老两国连续五年在澜湄水域联合开展渔政执法和水生生物增殖放流活动，活动现场销毁电鱼机 60 套、地笼 36 个，渔网 110 张、电拖网 1 副、迷魂阵 1 副；放生鱼苗胡子鲶 20 万尾，丝尾鳠 10 万尾，大鳞四须鲃 1.5 万尾，进一步促进了澜湄水生生物资源种群恢复，加强了中老双边合作，增进了两国人民友谊。活动结束后，两国执法人员乘 060 渔政执法船开展了渔政联合巡航执法，保障了增殖放流的效果（图 5）。

图 5　联合执法团队合影

（六）筹备建立澜湄流域渔业和水生态养护交流合作机制

受新冠肺炎疫情影响，原定于 2020 年 2 月召开的建立澜湄流域渔业和水生态养护交流合作机制的会议无法按期召开。会议筹备组已起草会议工作方案，澜湄流域渔业和水生态合作章程（草案）、备忘录、框架协议以及无锡宣言等相关文件，并通过邮件的方式与澜湄国家沟通交流，进一步完善合作机制建设。多次与国内有关单位和部门探讨筹建合作机制会议的相关工作，并组织国内专家学者研讨完善有关会议材料。

三、取得的成效

（一）经济效益

通过本项目实施，开展澜湄流域柬埔寨、中国、老挝、缅甸、泰国、越南六国渔业和水生态合作，建立澜湄流域渔业及水生态养护交流合作机制并逐步完善，有效提升六国渔业及水生态养护合作效率。同时，帮助湄公河流域国家提升水生态养护能力，为流域内渔业资源恢复和养护提供数据支撑，为澜湄国家渔业发展提供参考，避免不必要的投入及损失，具有一定经济效益。

（二）生态效益

通过本项目实施，有效提升澜湄六国水生态养护能力，联动保护澜湄流域水生态资源；采取联合执法的方式，能够有效取缔非法网具、打击非法捕捞活动，有效保护渔业及水生态资源；能够从理论与实际两方面提升澜湄国家水生生物保护水平，持续推进中外水生生物保护与渔业合作，生态效益显著。

（三）社会效益

本项目是落实澜湄合作机制的重要部署，综合考虑国内发展需要及湄公河国家需求，发挥中国资金、技术、人力资源等优势，推进中国与湄公河国家水生生物保护与渔业合作，提升社会公众对水域环境满意度及保护意识，宣传渔业及水生态养护、生物多样性保护知识，社会效益显著。

四、项目影响

本项目主要对以下两个方面产生影响：

（一）提升中国负责任的大国形象

本项目是遵循习近平外交思想，践行亲诚惠容周边外交理念，坚持义利相兼、以义为先的正确义利观，同湄公河国家共同努力的具体成果，是具体落实《澜湄合作五年行动计划（2018—2022）》的重要工作内容，是进一步加强澜湄水生态保护合作、分享中国在大河流域水生态保护及资源养护工作成果的重要举措。本项目主要是为流域人民谋幸福、为区域繁荣作贡献，其顺利实施有助于建立澜湄流域渔业和水生态养护交流合作平台，推动澜湄流域水生态保护和渔业资源养护工作，增进六国民众的友好感情。

（二）推动澜湄流域渔业可持续发展

本项目有利于提高澜湄流域国家水生态保护管理能力，提升相关国家管理人员、普通民众的水生生物保护意识，通过建立湄公江豚保护社区、发展生态旅游实现保护和利用协调发展，有力增进澜湄国家民生福祉，提升澜湄国家水生态保护的广度和成效，促进澜湄流域渔业可持续发展。

五、面临的困难与挑战

（一）新冠肺炎疫情影响项目执行效果

受新冠肺炎疫情影响，后续项目需要改变执行方式，如联合执法改为同步执法、培训由线下改为线上、湄公江豚考察及渔业资源调查将委托当地渔业工作者开展等，预计会对项目执行效果产生影响，且短期内无法改变。

（二）主客观因素影响项目执行进度

在项目执行期间，与各国间尚存在着计划执行度及沟通效率略低等问题。同时，澜湄国家气候复杂多变，执行考察可能存在雨季旱季交叉现象，增加了项目实施难度。

（三）技术研究局限性影响合作升级

标本及遗传样本等处理、鉴定分析途径及方式的不确定性，影响澜湄流域重要鱼类种质资源收集整理。同时，专业性研究主要集中在中国国内，针对澜湄流域的渔业资源、濒危水生生物资源保护和管理等方面的研究较为薄弱。渔业领域的合作处于分散状态，交流渠道尚未完全成熟，合作评价体系尚不完善，影响澜湄流域渔业和水生态养护交流合作机制的建立。

六、成功经验

同饮一江水，命运紧相连。自 2018 年澜湄流域水生生物保护及渔业合作项目实施以来，经受住国际地区风云变幻和新冠肺炎疫情考验，秉持民生为本，聚焦生物多样性保护，以生态为导向，以技术促发展，以合作求共赢，打造了协同联动的发展格局。澜湄流域六国携手共促水生态养护交流合作，为增进各国民众福祉、促进区域渔业可持续发展作出了重要贡献。

（一）以生态为导向

通过开展澜湄流域水生生物资源养护工作，提高了湄公江豚保护和水生生物资源养护能力，促进澜湄流域水生生物资源可持续利用，在发展的同时保护水生生物多样性，以生态为导向打造跨国绿色经济格局。

（二）以技术促发展

项目以实现共建绿色澜湄的目标，综合考虑澜湄国家水生态保护及资源养护需求，组建中国核心技术团队，重点在生物多样性保护等方面作出一系列研究，贡献一大批优秀成果，为务实合作赋予技术保障。

（三）以合作求共赢

澜湄六国地缘相接、人缘相亲、文缘相通。项目用实打实的行动、心连心的举措，坚持脚踏实地、不尚空谈、务实为先、民生为要的澜湄特色，持续有力推动澜湄流域水生态养护交流合作向更宽领域、更深层次发展，汇聚民智民力，互利共赢，共同走出一条绿色发展之路。

案例八　澜湄热带农业产业合作示范区项目

澜湄流域的国家和地区大部分属于热带或亚热带气候，农业为该区域传统支柱产业。虽有较好的自然资源禀赋，但该区域农业现代化水平较低，科技对农业增长贡献率不高。如何利用热区资源优势，提高热带农业产业综合生产能力、国际竞争力和可持续发展能力，推动传统农业向现代农业转型升级，是该区域面临的一大难题。澜湄热带农业产业合作示范区项目旨在通过建设区域热带农业产业合作示范区，从战略高度研究澜湄区域热带农业现代化的发展路径，使各国热作资源实现优势互补，打造新型跨国产业格局。

一、项目目标

通过与柬埔寨当地企业合作，采用中国成熟的水肥一体化灌溉技术和科学规范的农业产业化管理模式，发挥科研院所的科技资源优势，开展澜湄国家热带农业人才培育工作，带动当地香蕉、胡椒、椰子和芒果等产业发展及跨区域合作，推动澜湄国家农业农村经济共同发展，构建澜湄国家命运共同体。

示范区以建立"一核多园 N 基地"为主要目标。其中，一核是指绿洲农业发展（柬埔寨）有限公司位于柬埔寨桔井省的 20 万亩核心示范基地；多园是指遴选适应性强的热带特色农业品种，搭建生产要素相对齐全的全产业链经营管理团队，建设规模化和现代化产业示范园；N 基地是指引导澜湄区域的外资、中资和本土企业因地制宜建设规范化和标准化的农业生产基地。

二、项目活动

围绕澜湄热带特色农业产业开展系列技术交流合作。

（一）开展热带农业技术交流与人才培养

一是组织技术专家赴境外进行实地指导，先后组织十多批次、近 300 位主管领导、企业家、技术专家调研指导柬埔寨桔井省的核心示范基地，积极引导企业"走出去"。二是先后在中国海南省、柬埔寨举办 2 期澜湄区域热带农业人才培训班，组织澜湄各国的农业技术和管理人员参加了培训；三是举办 4 期中柬热带农业技术培训班，累计培训学员约 300 人次；四是承办 3 期胡椒高产技术培训活动，累计培训学员约 150 人次。

（二）建设农业产业合作核心示范基地

示范区以"政府引导、市场引领、企业为主、社会服务、农民受益"为指导思想，按照"一核多园 N 基地"的发展模式建设农业产业合作核心示范基地。截至 2020 年 5 月，已经建设完成 15 000 亩椰子产业合作核心示范基地（含 50 亩椰子种质资源苗圃），5 000 亩香蕉产业合作核心示范基地（图 1、图 2），1 000 亩胡椒产业合作核心示范基地（图 3），

图 1　香蕉产业合作核心示范基地

图 2　香蕉产业合作核心示范基地太阳能光电控水灌溉系统

10 000 亩橡胶产业核心示范基地，10 000 亩芒果产业合作核心示范基地，10 000 亩柚木产业合作核心示范基地，300 亩腰果产业合作核心示范基地。同期升级改造基础设施，平整 50 000 亩土地，购置 200 多台套农林机械，修建 200 多千米园区道路、20 000 米² 厂房、2 000 米² 办公及生活区，建设接入柬埔寨国家公共电网，建成中小型水库 5 座，旱季供水能力超过 2 000 万米³。

图 3　胡椒产业合作核心示范基地

（三）开展示范区生态保护

打造"生态保护＋农业开发"相结合的澜湄区域热带生态农业发展新模式，联合环保机构为示范区制定生态环境和生物多样性保护规划，划定生态保护红线，划定 12 万亩热带原始森林用于生态保育，8 万亩土地用于农业种植及水库、道路、加工区、办公生活区建设等，划定动植物保育生态走廊，划定斑点式开发模块，保持核心示范基地 60％以上的森林覆盖率、90％以上的植被覆盖率（图 4）。

图 4　示范区内受保护的野生动物

61

三、取得的成效

(一)热作产业地位确立,种植适宜区域明确

重新进行柬埔寨热作产业资源调查和区域规划,通过明确柬埔寨种植适宜区域,避免出现热作产业结构调整盲目趋同现象。加大了政府的引导力度,大力支持了农业支柱产业,如柬埔寨的椰子、香蕉、胡椒、芒果产业,形成以点带线、以线带面的全面发展格局。

(二)优良水果品种持续引进,种子品种不断改良

柬埔寨积极引进优良水果品种,优化种子品种结构,改变目前种质结构单一的局面。50亩椰子种质资源圃已经完成了苗圃建设和种子资源收集工作。加快了柬埔寨芒果、椰子等老果园的改造,大力推行现有的植株回缩矮化技术,促进产业升级,提高产品质量。加强了柬埔寨产后加工,通过开发高附加值产品,延长了产业链,积极抢占了国际市场,争取了更大的生存空间。

(三)标准化生产逐步开展,产业经营模式开始变革

改变了柬埔寨粗放经营的发展方式,形成了"企业+农户"的现代订单农业经营模式,实行品牌战略和产供销一体化,提高产品质量、降低市场成本,增强产品市场竞争力。逐步形成规范化的管理体系,进行统一标准管理、统一物资供应、统一品牌经营,打造了大型绿色农产品生产基地,培育具备国际竞争力的农业产业及农业企业,促进柬埔寨农业产业的标准化、产业化发展。形成了全产业链格局,围绕柬埔寨香蕉产业,先后吸引多家专业企业共同建设全产业链集群,形成了水肥一体化灌溉设施技术服务、有机肥料生产服务、物流运输服务、检验检疫食品安全服务、组培苗技术生产服务、纸箱包装袋服务等配套齐全的全产业链格局。

(四)基础设施建设逐渐完善,人才培育体系稳步构建

根据区域化布局和专业化生产的需要,示范区在内部完善相关硬件投资的同时,外部构建与完善培训运作系统。当前,15 000亩椰子产业合作核心示范基地已经完成了土地平整、灌溉挖塘蓄水、道路碾压、电力设施建设、生产用房建设等硬件投资,完成了椰子种苗育苗、挖坑定植、水肥

一体化灌溉设施铺设等工作。按照目标任务，稳步推进人才培育体系建设，将培训班工作与基地产业建设内外对接，逐步完善"一站式"培训体系。2020 年 3—12 月，共举办热带农业有害生物疫情监测、预警、综合防治等培训班 6 期。培训班以需求分析为导向，强化培训效果，加强方式创新，为澜湄国家热带农业人才培育工程整体建设打下了坚实的基础。

四、项目影响

（一）确立了农业科技合作在澜湄热带农业产业合作中的重要地位

通过与湄公河国家分享农业技术发展经验，推广优良品种、农业机械、栽培管理技术，部分品种增产 1 倍以上。通过举办农业技术与管理培训班，有力促进了澜湄国家热带农业技术合作，提升了当地农业生产力。

（二）拓宽了东盟国家与中国的农业合作领域

从热区农业产业合作发展到加工、仓储、物流、贸易等产业链各个环节，涉及粮食作物（水稻）、经济作物（橡胶、棕榈、木薯、甘蔗）等多种农产品，且呈迅速扩大趋势。这将有助于充分发挥澜湄各国的区位优势、产业优势，实现中国—东盟战略伙伴关系 2030 年愿景，促进澜湄国家内部资源、人力、资金更合理配置。推进基础设施、农业加工等领域的产业升级。

（三）带动当地农民就业，促进民间交流

中柬香蕉产业项目建成投产能为当地带来 60 亿元以上的劳务及关联消费收入，提供超过 10 万个就业岗位，为柬埔寨当地民生改善做出巨大贡献，使园区成为两国人民共同的美丽家园（图 5）。

五、面临的困难与挑战

（一）热带农产品加工发展缓慢

初级农产品附加值低，而经过二次深加工，这些农产品的附加值将大大增加，在价格方面将占有较大优势。除了技术原因，中国和湄公河各国在农产品加工方面均没有足够重视，热带农产品不加工或粗加工多，精加

图 5　为柬埔寨当地提供就业机会改善民生

工少，企业能耗、物耗高，产出效益低下。

（二）建立全程质量可追溯系统存在困难

急需项目支持柬埔寨建设农产品质量检验检疫中心，建立全程质量可追溯系统。通过做好产品检验检疫和过程质量监控，确保农产品符合出口国和进口国的质量安全要求。

六、成功经验

（一）加快推进产业落地

扩大技术合作范围，加强政研企对接，使得科研成果成功向产业规模投资转化，实验室技术得以规模化量产，提升了产业空间与价值。此外，柬埔寨通过充分学习利用澜湄国家先进的热带农业科学技术，加强技术创新，加快发展热带农产品品种以及品种改良工作，打造国际品牌。通过应用信息技术，更好地引导生产适销对路的农产品，增加农民收入。

（二）发挥学员纽带作用，搭建交流合作桥梁

以培训促合作，项目综合效益明显。通过实施农业技术培训，充分发挥项目综合效益，直接推动科研院所与澜湄当地企业有效对接，打造产业合作的总体格局。此外，项目以技术培训和回访调研有机结合为基础，开展针对性的人才需求与合作机制等研究，进一步从理论和实践层面推动澜

湄热带农业合作的可持续发展。

（三）保护生态环境，打造农业与生态协调发展新态势

通过打造"生态保护＋农业开发"相结合的农业合作开发模式，既促进了当地农业产业的发展，又保护了当地的生态环境，使农业产业可持续发展理念在当地得到极大认可，为长期有效合作奠定了重要基础。

第三篇 | 能力建设类

案例九　澜湄国家人力资源合作开发体系建设及培训项目

一、项目目标

随着澜湄合作机制的推进和深化，各领域的高质量合作对人力资源支撑提出了更高要求，加强澜湄国家人力资源开发合作的重要意义日益凸显。近年来，澜湄农业合作能力建设项目稳步开展，主要包括以下内容：

澜沧江—湄公河流域国家热带农业人才培育工程项目，以开展农业产业管理与技术培训为主，同时围绕人力资源合作、农业科技减贫、支撑企业"走出去"、培训基地建设、人才需求机制研究等内容，推动澜湄流域国家农业发展和乡村振兴，打造澜湄农业合作培训样板工程。

跨境动物疫病实验室诊断检测技术培训，旨在主动服务和积极对接"一带一路"倡议，为有序推进云南边境口蹄疫控制区试点工作和家畜跨境流动规范化，建立安全贸易走廊，促进畜禽及其产品合法贸易提供技术支撑。

湄公河流域国家沼气技术培训班聚焦沼气技术，推动使其成为区域可持续发展的重要手段。项目设计了讲座、现场实践、参观示范、企业考察和经验分享等活动。设立并成功完成了 2 个后续项目，包括联合国工业发展组织支持的在柬埔寨皇家大学开展的"柬埔寨商业沼气培训班"，和 77 国集团佩罗基金（PGTF）支持的在菲律宾开展的"偏远农村地区安装和示范玻璃钢消化池项目"。培训项目成为相互交流与推进后续合作的重要平台和窗口。

澜湄国家农药风险管理研修班项目，以加强澜湄各国在农药风险管理方面的经验交流、提高区域农药风险管理能力、落实"一带一路"倡议为主旨，通过分享交流澜湄各国在农药风险管控领域共同面临的风险和挑战、中国农药风险管控工作所取得的进展与方法，为今后澜湄国家不断加强农药等相关领域的合作，提高区域农药风险管理能力，促进澜湄区域农业的可持续发展提供助力。

二、项目活动

(一) 实施六期澜沧江—湄公河流域国家农业产业管理与技术培训

2018 年 5—9 月，实施了热带农业有害生物疫情监测、预警、综合防治培训班，热带农产品质量安全标准与检测技术研修班，热带特色经济作物生产与加工技术培训班，现代农业产业园区与农业信息化培训班，热带畜禽规模化养殖与饲料作物种植技术培训班（图 1）和"一村一品"现代农业可持续发展研修班，共 6 期培训，每期培训 10 天，共培训来自柬埔寨、老挝、缅甸、泰国和越南等国政府机构、高等院校、科研院所和农业企业的各类管理和技术人员 124 人。

图 1　热带畜禽规模化养殖与饲料作物种植技术培训班结业合影

培训以技术需求为导向，邀请具有丰富国际合作经验的专家学者授课，并带领学员参观考察各类示范基地、体验中国传统文化，为澜沧江—湄公河流域国家热带农业人才培育工程整体建设打下了坚实的基础。

(二) 开展跨境动物疫病实验室诊断检测技术培训

2018 年 6 月 11—24 日，在云南昆明、西双版纳和曲靖等州市举办完成澜湄合作专项基金项目"澜沧江—湄公河国家跨境动物疫病实验室诊断检测技术培训与示范"的"请进来"培训任务（图 2）。老挝、缅甸、泰国和越南四国 12 名实验室技术人员应邀参加培训。

图 2　跨境动物疫病实验室诊断检测技术培训合影

2018 年 8 月 26 日至 9 月 7 日，应老挝农林部家畜和水产局邀请，云南省畜牧兽医科学院组建 3 名技术专家组成的"赴老挝开展跨境动物疫病实验室诊断检测技术培训与示范团"，赴老挝万象和沙耶武里省开展跨境动物疫病实验室诊断检测技术培训与示范（图 3），为期 12 天，培训老方兽医技术人员 25 人，完成澜湄合作专项基金项目"走出去"部分交流合作任务。

图 3　老挝万象、沙耶武里口蹄疫实验室诊断检测技术培训

应缅甸农业、畜牧与灌溉部畜牧兽医局计划统计国际和信息技术处邀请，由云南省畜牧兽医科学院组建技术专家团队，于 2018 年 12 月 4—12 日，赴缅甸和泰国执行澜湄国家跨境动物疫病防控技术"走出去"交流合作任务。结合云南省对缅甸援助项目缅甸牛口蹄疫诊断检测技术培训，技术专家团队于 2019 年 1 月 6—19 日赴缅甸仰光、内比都举办牛口蹄疫诊断技术培训，培训缅甸仰光、内比都、曼德勒三地技术人员 23 人，并签订实验室合作协议。

（三）筹建湄公河流域国家沼气技术培训班

2018 年湄公河流域国家沼气技术培训班，由中国农业农村部沼气科学研究所培训与信息研究中心培训部具体负责。项目制定了详细周密的安全保卫工作实施方案，拟定了国际培训班突发事件应急预案、培训岗位职责。向联合国工业发展组织、亚太沼气联盟等国际民间团体推送招生通知，征集候选学员，甄选具有专业基础和相关领域工作经验的人员作为最终人选。

培训班最终于 2018 年 3 月 21 日至 4 月 3 日在成都成功举办，对来自柬埔寨、缅甸、老挝、泰国、越南五国的 21 名学员进行了为期 14 天的培训。具体教学过程中，根据培训班的时间、主题以及学员需求，制定培训日程，邀请了具有丰富教学和工作经验的专家作为授课教师，并积极督促教材制作和更新。

（四）举办澜湄国家农药风险管理研修班

2019 年 7 月 15 日至 8 月 4 日，举办澜湄国家农药风险管理研修班，历时三周，培训和参观考察活动分别在中国北京、广西和云南进行。主要培训内容包括专家课堂授课、参观中国农业农村部农药检定所实验室、考察农药企业、参观生态农业产业园以及开展文化交流等（图 4、图 5）。参加培训的 28 名学员分别来自泰国、柬埔寨、越南、缅甸和老挝 5 个国家的相关农业部门和科研院校。

在授课交流环节，联合各授课专家和合作单位为培训班制定了科学详细的授课计划，内容涵盖中国农药管理政策与环境风险控制、中国农药风险管理方法、中国农药登记审批流程、农药残留、生物多样性与病虫害防治、植物病虫害生物防治研究新进展，多维度、多层面保证了授课的广度

图 4　专家与学员探讨交流

图 5　参观农药企业实验室

和深度，丰富了学员的农药知识。

　　参观考察环节，组织学员到企业进行实地调研，并赴广西南宁、北海、云南昆明及周边市县进行参观考察和学习交流，使学员们对中国的农药企业、生态农业、绿色防控等农药风险管理的具体方法有了更直观、更深入的了解和认识。

三、取得的成效

（一）扩充了农业人力资源，打造了澜湄合作朋友圈

中国于 2018 年起实施澜沧江—湄公河流域国家热带农业人才培育工

程项目，开展了 6 期农业产业管理与技术培训，共计培训 124 名澜湄国家农业管理官员、农业技术专家和涉农企业管理者，建设了澜沧江—湄公河流域国家热带农业人才培训基地。开发了 13 个精品培训课程，遴选了 9 处培训实践基地，建立了 1 个澜湄培训数据管理系统，完善了培训管理机制与配套制度，并且和柬埔寨劳工与职业培训部签订关于科技人才培训的合作意向书。

（二）构建了可持续合作交流机制，促进了合作交流常态化

通过签订合作协议、建立人员互访机制、调研人才发展情况、后续人员跟踪培训等方式，促进澜湄各国合作交流常态化。以此建立了基层农技推广人员长期、可持续的合作交流机制。如中国云南省畜牧兽医科学院与缅甸内比都国家口蹄疫实验室签订技术合作协议，促进了中缅跨境动物疫病防控双边合作，提高了云南在国际动物卫生领域的影响。受柬埔寨学员邀请，赴柬埔寨举办联合国工业发展组织支持的商业化沼气技术培训班第一期（2018 年 5 月 25 日至 6 月 1 日）和第二期（2018 年 6 月 25 日至 7 月 5 日），有效延伸了相关培训项目，以此完成对湄公河国家学员的技术交流、成果示范、企业推介、经验分享，保障各国农业合作机制的稳定性、可持续性。

四、项目影响

（一）优化了澜湄国家农业人力资源结构

基于"授人以鱼不如授人以渔"的人才培训理念，中国相关机构向各国公众开设培训课程，进行农业科技知识文化和专业技能的普及与示范推广，在推进"一带一路"倡议和构建澜湄国家命运共同体的大背景下，对接湄公河各国发展战略，在澜湄合作框架下构建人力资源开发合作机制，大力推进中国与湄公河国家之间相互访学、职业教育、政府和企业间人员交流培训等领域的人力资源开发合作，促进了澜湄区域的人才信息互联互通。

（二）通过培训和后续沟通强化合作意向

澜湄各国学员积极沟通，促成了彼此合作方案备忘录，在提升互联互通效率的同时，达成了在合作研究、能力建设、技术示范、沟通交流等方

面开展合作的意向；通过后续的学员培训交流，加深了对彼此的了解与信任。

（三）强化澜湄国家命运共同体意识

培训活动期间，澜湄国家培训班与研修班创新组织联谊活动，澜湄各国学员积极参与，展示了各国民俗风情，增进了彼此友谊，激发了学员的学习兴趣和交流热情。在此过程中，提高了澜湄各国学员的澜湄国家命运共同体意识、增进了理解、加深了友谊，为澜湄农业领域后续合作奠定了坚实基础。

五、面临的困难与挑战

（一）交流合作机制不畅通

如在合作方式上，跨国调研、技术交流受到空间限制，虽然一些国际组织已经开始通过线上交流对合作项目进行总结、对合作趋势进行探讨，但部分领域交流活动有限。另外，相关研修班在招生阶段面临较大压力，考虑到每个国家审核程序以及培训周期，加上每年暑期中国涉外培训集中举办，出现了生源不足的问题。澜湄区域内统一协调的动物流动管理和疫病联防联控合作机制不畅，开展跨境动物疫病防控合作与交流存在一定的风险和不确定性。

（二）不确定性风险显著增加

来华培训与境外培训期间，学员可能会受到环境、疾病、饮食等不确定因素的影响，从而可能造成人身安全风险。

六、成功经验

（一）提升产业合作示范基地多功能特征

打造了一个"有干头、有看头、有说头"的样板基地，发挥基地人才培育、科技示范功能。

（二）形成基层农技推广人员能力建设品牌

规划基层农技推广人员能力提升培育工程，建立长效合作发展机制，促进培育工作的可持续发展，逐步形成体系，打造品牌。

(三) 加强管理，保证培训质量

授课过程中，提前谋划，积极筹备，邀请授课专家、确定参观路线，安排专家、学员、企业负责人以及农民进行会谈交流，并提高后勤服务水平，营造良好的培训环境，确保培训的积极效果，保证培训班质量。

(四) 加强联络，拓宽合作渠道

积极协调学员与企业、科研机构的联络与接洽，为深化合作牵线搭桥，并协助学员了解到华留学、科研等信息，扩大了培训影响，充实了项目成果。

(五) 注重后期跟踪和交流

发挥培训与研修班的积极效应，加强后期政府和企业的交流与合作，共同促进澜湄区域的粮食安全和农业的可持续发展。

Report on the Development of Lancang–Mekong Agricultural Cooperation 2020

Foreign Economic Cooperation Center, Ministry of
Agriculture and Rural Affairs, P.R.C

China Agriculture Press
Beijing

澜沧江—湄公河农业合作发展报告 2020

Report on the Development of Lancang-Mekong
Agricultural Cooperation 2020

Editorial Board

Preface

In March 2016, China proposed the establishment of the Lancang-Mekong Cooperation Special Fund (LMCSF) project at the First Lancang-Mekong Cooperation (LMC) Leaders' Meeting. It will provide US $ 300 million in five years to support small and medium-sized cooperation projects in six countries in the Lancang-Mekong basin. Agriculture is one of the five priority areas of LMC. With the support of LMCSF, member countries have implemented various types of agricultural cooperation projects such as policy dialogue, industrial upgrading, and capacity building.

The implementation of LMCSF agricultural projects has significantly promoted the development of agricultural cooperation in this area. The projects have supported the establishment of multi-level and multi-subject exchange and dialogue platforms for the agricultural departments of the six Lancang-Mekong countries, and promotes strategic alignment, policy exchange and experience sharing. The projects have also supported technical exchanges and cooperation in key industries such as rice, natural rubber, specialty fruits and vegetables, fisheries, and animal husbandry. The quality and efficiency of the agricultural industry in the Lancang-Mekong region have been improved. In addition, the projects have supported the joint construction of agricultural technology training centers, carried out domestic and foreign trainings and exchanges, and improved the comprehensive capabilities of the agricultural technicians in Lancang-Mekong region.

In order to comprehensively evaluate the role of LMCSF agricultural projects in supporting and promoting Lancang-Mekong agricultural cooperation, the *Report* summarizes typical cases since the implementation of LMCSF agricultural projects. Based on this, the *Report* sums up and analyzes the main models, practices and effects of the projects. Furthermore, the *Report* seeks to provide prospects for future planning and design of LMCSF agricultural projects, and provide a scientific basis to better make use of LMCSF and other resources, promote the sustainable development of the Lancang-Mekong agricultural cooperation and enhance the effectiveness and quality of the implementation of the LMC projects.

Editorial Board
November, 2021

Contents ////////////

I

General Report

Overview of Lancang-Mekong Agricultural Cooperation Projects

On March 23, 2016, the First LMC Leaders' Meeting was successfully held in Sanya, Hainan. With the theme of "Shared River, Shared Future", the leaders of Cambodia, China, Laos, Myanmar, Thailand, and Vietnam announced the launch of Lancang-Mekong Cooperation to jointly build a community of shared future of peace and prosperity among Lancang-Mekong countries. At this meeting, China proposed the establishment of the LMCSF, and planned to provide US$ 300 million in five years to support small and medium-sized cooperation projects in the six Lancang-Mekong countries. From 2017 to 2020, the LMCSF successively supported nearly 400 projects. Since agriculture is one of the five priority areas of Lancang-Mekong cooperation, member countries have implemented more than 100 agricultural cooperation projects.

The Lancang-Mekong agricultural cooperation projects focus on the agricultural development needs of Cambodia, China, Laos, Myanmar, Thailand and Vietnam. They have vigorously promoted closer agricultural exchanges between member countries and achieved mutual promotion and common progress by strengthening cooperation in various aspects including agricultural policy dialogues, agricultural industry upgrading, agricultural trade and investment promotion, and capacity building. The projects have made positive contributions in promoting the protection and utilization of agricultural resources and improving food security and food nutrition in

Lancang-Mekong region. In addition, the projects have contributed to promoting the implementation of the United Nations 2030 Agenda for Sustainable Development in Agriculture and realizing rural revitalization and common development.

1 Brief Introduction to Lancang-Mekong Agricultural Cooperation Projects

From 2017 to 2020, LMCSF supported the implementation of more than 100 agricultural cooperation projects. Among them, nearly 70 projects were implemented by Mekong countries and nearly 40 projects by China. The projects involved diverse agricultural fields, covering planting (rice, rubber, banana, coffee, fruits and vegetables, cassava, bamboo, etc.), breeding industry (goats, silkworms, etc.), seed industry, agro-product processing, pest control, agro-product trade, rural development, poverty reduction, etc.

The Ministry of Agriculture and Rural Affairs of China organized and implemented nearly 30 LMCSF projects from 2017 to 2020. The projects mainly focused on the fields of construction of the Lancang-Mekong agricultural support system, multi-field platform construction, technology demonstration in key industries (including rice, rubber, fisheries, etc.), agricultural production infrastructure construction, and technical personnel training.

2 Main Types of Lancang-Mekong Agricultural Cooperation Projects

Implemented Lancang-Mekong agricultural cooperation projects mainly include three types: policy dialogue, industrial upgrading, and capacity building.

2.1 Policy Dialogue Projects

Policy dialogue projects aimed to establish a multi-level and multi-themed exchange and dialogue mechanism, to promote practical cooperation in the fields of technology and industry, which would eventually lead to the strategic alignment, policy exchange and experience sharing in the Lancang-Mekong region. Specific measures were to build and upgrade policy dialogue platforms and organize exchange activities, etc.

According to the different participants, the main practices of policy dialogue projects are as follows.

2.1.1 The Construction of Cooperation and Supporting Systems

The projects were mainly carried out by government departments and agricultural research institutes. With the support from the Lancang-Mekong Agricultural Cooperation Center, while maintaining the normal operation of the Lancang-Mekong agricultural cooperation mechanism, the projects built cooperation and exchange platforms in fields of agricultural technology, investment, and trade, constructed agricultural cooperation and supporting systems with the comparative advantages of Lancang-Mekong countries to provide strategic support for the interconnection of agricultural cooperation, the exchange of ecological resources, and the mutual assistance of economic resources between member countries. The agricultural cooperation and supporting systems construction projects that have been carried out can support, on the one hand, the operation of the LMC Joint Working Group on Agriculture mechanism and provide as a bridge for the communication of agricultural policies, and the design of agricultural development strategies of member countries. On the other hand, Lancang-Mekong Agricultural Extension and Information Platform (AEIP) was constructed to release information, promote agricultural technologies, provide expert Q&A, and perform as a farmers' exchange forum. It is also a service platform to promote the localization of agricultural technologies and information in member countries. The projects supported the establishment of good cooperative relations among agricultural departments of central as well as local governments, key

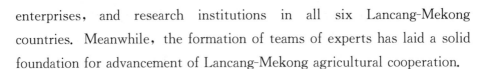

enterprises, and research institutions in all six Lancang-Mekong countries. Meanwhile, the formation of teams of experts has laid a solid foundation for advancement of Lancang-Mekong agricultural cooperation.

2. 1. 2 Regional All-round Agricultural Cooperation

These projects relied on media promotion, especially TV shows. By building a multi-national mainstream TV media cooperation platform or alliance, the projects actively promoted the scientific and technological knowledge and development experience of agriculture in the six Lancang-Mekong countries, and promoted multi-party media exchanges. The all-round agricultural cooperation projects in Lancang-Mekong region have used the media of member countries as a bridge to actively disseminate information on agricultural science and technology, rural development, and farmers' lives of the Lancang-Mekong basin countries, which has gradually encouraged farmers to make use of the information from the TV shows. By far, it has adapted and produced 60 episodes of *China Farm*, filmed and produced 32 new episodes, and produced 6 bilingual promotional videos of *China Farm—Lancang-Mekong Action*. The programs have effectively promoted the exchanges between China and the Mekong countries in agricultural field.

2. 2 Industry Upgrading Projects

The industrial upgrading projects focused on supporting the development of the Lancang-Mekong region's characteristic and advantageous agricultural industries, such as coffee, rice, natural rubber, specialty fruits and vegetables, and fisheries. They carried out production and quality improvement projects, jointly constructed high-quality varieties test demonstration bases, technology promotion centers and technological cooperation demonstration parks, built agricultural technology promotion and information exchange platforms and ecological conservation exchange and cooperation mechanism, etc.

The main practices of industrial upgrading projects are as follows:

2.2.1 Industrial Upgrading Through the Establishment of Experimental Demonstration Bases

Through establishing experimental demonstration bases designated for experimental demonstration of agricultural technology, high-quality varieties, and management models, the quality, efficiency, and upgrading of the local agricultural industry have been promoted. Typical projects included: Myanmar Coffee Production and Quality Improvement, Demonstration of Intergration of Rubber Tree Cultivation and Processing Technology in Lancang-Mekong Countries, Demonstration Zone for Cooperation on Tropical Agricultural Industrialization of Lancang-Mekong Area, etc. Among them, the Demonstration Zone Project for Cooperation on Tropical Agricultural Industrialization of Lancang-Mekong Area has built a 1,000 mu of coconut industry cooperation demonstration base in Cambodia which has improved the technology, management, and standards of both parties.

2.2.2 Industry Upgrading Through Personnel Training

Through technical training in production, management, sale, etc. in agricultural field, both the skill level of agricultural employees and the soft power of production and operation of local agriculture have been improved. These indirectly led to the upgrading of the industries. For example, personnel trainings were carried out in both Myanmar Coffee Production and Quality Improvement Project and Demonstration of Intergration of Rubber Tree Cultivation and Processing Technology in Lancang-Mekong Countries, which has effectively promoted the upgrading of the agricultural industries. Among them, Myanmar Coffee Production and Quality Improvement Project has conducted professional coffee production training for 14 times in Myanmar's Chin State, Kachin State, Shan State, Mandalay and Magway Provinces and trained 1,639 trainees, which has greatly improved the technical level of the local personnel.

2.2.3 Protecting Ecology to Achieve Sustainable Development of Agriculture

By promoting green production technologies in agricultural

production, enhancing ecological protection regulation, launching exchanges of agricultural ecological protection, regional ecological protection capabilities were improved and the coordinated development of agriculture and ecology was promoted. This could eventually ensure sustainable development of agriculture. For example, Lancang-Mekong Sub-regional Rice Green Yield-increasing Technology Experiment and Demonstration Project has promoted the green development of agricultural production through the application and promotion of green yield-increasing technology. Through the establishment of the water ecological conservation and fisheries cooperation mechanism in the Lancang-Mekong River Basin and the launch of China-Laos joint law enforcement activities, Aquatic Animal Protection and Fishery Cooperation Project has significantly promoted the conservation of aquatic animal resources in the Lancang-Mekong River Basin.

2. 3 Capability Building Projects

Capacity building projects were guided by transferring agricultural professional skills and knowledge. These projects strived to improve the skills of agricultural officials, experts, technicians, and young backbones in Lancang-Mekong countries. These projects have built agricultural technology training centers, held various levels of personnel training activities, and promoted the exchange of agricultural talents.

The main practices of capacity building projects are as follows:

2. 3. 1 Long-term Projects on Agricultural Professional and Technical Personnel Capacity Improvement

Trainings of agricultural production and skill were carried out in the agricultural production base established through cooperation between the two parties, which eventually trained a group of agricultural technicians to make them can understand agriculture, operating and management. For example, the Agricultural Industry Management and Technology Training for the countries along the Lancang-Mekong River. Establishing the coconut industry cooperation demonstration base was not only for agricultural production, but also for the training of agricultural technology promotion personnel, which has greatly improved the agricultural technology level of the participants.

2.3.2　Short-term Projects on Agricultural Professional and Technical Personnel Training

Through lectures, experiments, inspections and other teaching activities in professional agricultural fields, technical exchanges, achievement demonstrations, enterprise promotion, experience sharing, etc. among Lancang-Mekong countries were realized. For example, Transboundary Animal Disease (TAD) Laboratory Diagnosis and Testing Technical Training, Training Course on Biogas Technology, and Capacity Building Seminar on Pesticide Risk Management for Lancang-Mekong Countries were all improving professional skills in the form of short-term trainings.

3　Achievements of Lancang-Mekong Agricultural Cooperation Projects

Since the implementation of Lancang-Mekong agricultural cooperation projects, Cambodia, China, Laos, Myanmar, Thailand, and Vietnam have worked together. Also, governments, research institutes, enterprises and agricultural business entities of member countries actively interacted with each other to improve cooperation plans, and strengthened practical cooperation. With the support of LMCSF, a series of agricultural projects benefiting people's livelihood have been implemented. The degree of cooperation has gradually deepened and the areas of cooperation have gradually expanded. In general, it has achieved practical results in five aspects: cooperation mechanism construction, technical exchange and cooperation, human resource empowerment, industrial cooperation and innovation, and regional welfare sharing.

3.1 Improvement of Lancang-Mekong Agricultural Cooperation Mechanism System

The existing projects mainly adopted the following two methods to establish and continuously improve the support system of Lancang-Mekong agricultural cooperation.

3.1.1 Multi-level Exchange and Cooperation Mechanism System

The projects established a multi-level and multi-domain mechanism structure including government agencies, scientific research institutions, experts and technical staff in various fields. This mechanism conducted communication, consultation and decision-making on cooperation issues such as policy dialogues, technical exchanges, capacity building, information exchanges, and joint research among Lancang-Mekong countries to ensure the implementation of the work plans generated by Lancang-Mekong Cooperation Agricultural Joint Working Group. Relying on the rich agricultural resource endowments of the countries in the Mekong sub-region, the mechanism aimed to build Lancang-Mekong agricultural development advantageous areas and explore cooperation in agricultural projects. By making full use of the agricultural resources in the Lancang-Mekong region, the advantages of agricultural resources were complemented and the comprehensive agricultural production capacity was improved.

3.1.2 Pragmatic Cooperation

There are differences in agricultural production methods and technologies in the six Lancang-Mekong countries, and the cultures of the countries are also significantly different. By strengthening media promotion and cooperation between Lancang-Mekong countries, the concept of Lancang-Mekong agricultural cooperation was spread. For example, multiple agricultural programs for topics of science and technology or rich experience have been adapted and produced. The projects also filmed the policies and activities of governments, agricultural enterprises and other actors in the Mekong countries. On the one hand, the concept of regional agricultural cooperation has been enhanced by helping farmers in Lancang-Mekong regions to master practical agricultural techniques as well as understand the degree and effectiveness of the implementation of the projects. On the other hand, these projects have strengthened people's recognition of Lancang-Mekong cooperation projects, which effectively promoted cultural exchanges among Lancang-Mekong countries and formed a foundation for agricultural connectivity and people's harmony. Both the breadth and depth of the Lancang-Mekong cooperation system were ensured.

3. 2   Deepening of Technical Exchanges and Cooperation

The exchange of science and technology, education and talents has always been an important area of cooperation in the Lancang-Mekong region. Through exchange and cooperation in the field of agricultural technology, Lancang-Mekong countries have established technology cooperation research and development platforms as well as technology testing and demonstration bases. It has promoted the promotion and application of excellent crop varieties, technologies, agricultural machinery, and agricultural materials in Lancang-Mekong countries. The achievements can be summarized in the following four areas.

3. 2. 1   Technical Exchange and Cooperation in Food Crop

By holding regular project promotion exchange meetings, progress of the project could be monitored timely to improve execution efficiency. For example, Lancang-Mekong Sub-regional Rice Green Yield-increasing Technology Experiment and Demonstration Project, through the implementation of experimental introduction of rice varieties and technologies, as well as the assembling and popularization of large-scale green yield-increasing technologies suitable for local rice production, yield and income of rice green production in neighboring countries have been increases.

3.2.2　Technical Exchange and Cooperation in Specialty Crop

Through the implementation of Demonstration of Intergration of Rubber Tree Cultivation and Processing Technology in Lancang-Mekong Countries, the high-yield and high-efficiency comprehensive cultivation management technology of rubber plantations were demonstrated and promoted, which has provided technical guidance for scientific research institutes, production units and farmers in Lancang-Mekong countries. Myanmar Rural Development and Vegetable Cultivation Technology Transfer Project carried out vegetable cultivation technology exchange activities, which has provided technical support for the efficient and high-quality development of the vegetable industry.

3.2.3　Technical Exchange and Cooperation in Cash Crop

Through the construction of Banana Seedling Breeding Platform and the Standardized Planting Demonstration Platform, Cambodia's local banana resources have been collected, preserved, and evaluated, by which high-quality and special banana resources have been selected to provide breeding materials for subsequent variety improvement. Lancang-Mekong tuber processing technology and equipment research and development platform project has greatly promoted the development of tuber processing industries in China, Laos, Vietnam, Myanmar, etc.

3.2.4　Technical Exchange and Cooperation in Fisheries

Through the implementation of the Lancang-Mekong Aquatic Animal Protection and Fishery Cooperation Project, targeted trainings have been conducted on the professional skills required by the relevant fishery during the inspection and observation process. At the same time, more effective protection measures have been implemented for endangered aquatic species, which have improved the capability of protecting aquatic organisms.

3.3　Improvement on Human Resources Cultivation System

The development of agriculture in the Lancang-Mekong region is inseparable from science and technology, let alone the support of human resources. Exchanges of information and personnel are mainly carried out in the form of exchange activities, forums, and seminars. Human resources were empowered and talent training system was built through the direct implementation of specific projects for improving business quality and knowledge of agricultural operating. The agricultural exchanges between Lancang-Mekong countries have been further strengthened, which has provided solid human capital support for Lancang-Mekong agricultural cooperation.

3.3.1 Technical Trainings

For example, with the Talent Training Project for Lancang-Mekong Countries as the main body, several agricultural industry management and technology trainings for the countries along the Lancang-Mekong River have been held. These courses have trained agricultural management officials, agricultural technical experts and managers of agricultural-related enterprises in Lancang-Mekong countries. The trainings mainly covered topics such as pest epidemic monitoring and prevention, quality and safety cooperation of agricultural products, production and processing of tropical economic crops, agricultural cooperation parks and agricultural informatization, tropical livestock and poultry breeding and feed planting, etc. On the one hand, green technology models with high-quality and high-efficiency that meet the requirements of "resource conservation, increased production and efficiency, ecological environmental protection, quality and safety" were promoted, which has improved the professional skills of technical promoting personnel. On the other hand, the knowledge level of practitioners in different fields has been improved in the trainings. The courses improved the close integration of industry, university and research, which have promoted the sharing and dissemination of relevant research results. This has enabled practitioners in Lancang-Mekong countries to obtain corresponding professional knowledge while achieving huge project benefits and influence.

3.3.2 Establishment of Scientific and Technological Demonstration Bases

The agricultural science and technology demonstration bases have become agricultural science and technology demonstration service platforms that integrate various functions such as demonstration, technical guidance, and farmer training. It has played an important role in comprehensively improving the level of agricultural technology and promoting the agricultural development in Lancang-Mekong countries. For example, Demonstration of Integration of Rubber Tree Cultivation and Processing Technology in Lancang-Mekong Countries provided rubber tree cultivation and processing technology trainings. The level of rubber production and processing and the professional level of local rubber production in the five Lancang-Mekong countries has been improved. In addition, the Lancang-Mekong country human resources cooperative development system was established to focus on improving the ability and quality of grass-roots agricultural technology promoting personnel and updating their knowledge. It has greatly promoted the construction of grassroots agricultural technology promoting team and improved the grassroots agricultural technology promoting capabilities of the Lancang-Mekong countries.

3.4 Agricultural Industry Cooperation and Innovation

Now, Lancang-Mekong industrial cooperation projects are developing in clusters. It has played an important role in promoting the quality and efficiency of the industry by strengthening industrial technology exchanges and innovating agriculture and industry cooperation. Meanwhile, green, efficient, and sustainable development of the industry has been promoted through the construction of ecological protection projects.

3.4.1 Ensuring Economic and Social Benefits

Lancang-Mekong agricultural cooperation projects covered multiple fields including rice, buckwheat, tuber, natural rubber, bean, banana, coconut, pepper, lemongrass, and fishery. It fully utilized the comparative advantages of Lancang-Mekong countries' agricultural resources and technologies, and promoted large-scale, standardized, and simplified high-yielding cultivation in Lancang-Mekong countries, which has led to the improvement of product quality. Meanwhile, production costs have been significantly reduced, and the anti-risk capability of farmers and production companies has been improved. The advantages of the industries in each region were obvious, which laid a solid foundation for economic and social benefits. On the other hand, simultaneous advancement of multiple projects helped ensuring the durability of expected benefits, and played an important role in promoting the industrial upgrading of agriculture in Lancang-Mekong countries.

3. 4. 2 A New Model of Industrial Upgrading with Technology as a Breakthrough

Most of the Lancang-Mekong agricultural cooperation projects used technological cooperation as a breakthrough to gradually transform from cooperation in technologies to cooperation in the entire agricultural industry chain, which has led to industrial transformation and upgrading. For example, the Lancang-Mekong Sub-regional Rice Green Yield-increasing Technology Experiment and Demonstration Project has formed a model of combining experiment and demonstration bases and comprehensive rice planting models through the introduction of China's mature technologies of seedling raising, planting, water and fertilizer management, green prevention and management of diseases and pests, etc. It helped the upgrading of production, sales, and management models of traditional industries, and further promoted agricultural industrialization, and accelerated the agricultural modernization.

3. 5 Sharing of Welfare in the Lancang-Mekong Region

The Lancang-Mekong agricultural cooperation projects have created a variety of cooperation and exchange modes such as policy, investment, technology, etc. , which covered multiple fields including planting, breeding, processing, and agricultural technology. It has laid a solid foundation for the development of welfare sharing and an integrated structure.

3.5.1 Regional Development and Increased Income of Local Farmers

The Lancang-Mekong agricultural cooperation projects have provided technical support for farmers to increase production and income in Lancang-Mekong region by improving their agricultural technology levels. For example: by applying and promoting green yield-increasing technology, the project has introduced, tested and screened new rice varieties with high quality, high yield, good resistance, and strong adaptability, which has provided germplasm guarantee for improving the quality and yield of rice in Lancang-Mekong sub-region. By improving the yield and quality of agro-products, the market competitiveness of rice in this region has been improved, and the income of farmers in the region has increased significantly. It also provided decision-making guarantees for income-increasing for the farmers through the establishment of policy systems and mechanisms. Since the project was initiated at the grassroots level, agricultural management and scientific and technical personnel could gain a deeper understanding of the development of agriculture and farmers in the project base. It provided a basis for decision-making to better capture the interests of local farmers and promote agricultural exchanges and cooperation.

3.5.2 Regional Development and Economic Benefits

By promoting the scale and standardization of the agricultural industry, the quality and efficiency of agro-products have been improved. Demonstration Zone Project for Cooperation on Tropical Agricultural Industrialization of Lancang-Mekong Area used the modern order-based agricultural business model of "enterprise+farmer" to implement brand strategy and production, supply and marketing integration strategy to improve product quality, reduce market costs, and enhance product market competitiveness. A standardized management system consisting of unified standardized management, material supply and brand management was formed, which has led to the establishment of a large-scale green agricultural product production base. Also, a number of internationally competitive agricultural industries and enterprises were created, which has promoted the standardization and industrialization of agricultural industry. It enhanced the international competitiveness of agro-products and promoted the international trade.

3.5.3　Regional Development and Ecological Benefits

The implementation of the project pays attention to agricultural ecological protection and promotes the reduction of agricultural inputs and green production. The efforts of protecting ecological environment in Lancang-Mekong region have been improved, and the damage to the ecological environment has been effectively reduced. In addition, by creating an agricultural cooperative development model that combines "ecological protection + agricultural development", it has not only promoted the development of local agricultural industry, but also protected local ecological environment. The concept of sustainable development of agriculture has been greatly recognized since the ecological benefits were significant, which has laid an important foundation for long-term effective cooperation.

4　Prospects for the Planning and Designing of Lancang-Mekong Agricultural Cooperation Projects

On the basis of strengthening policy dialogues among Lancang-Mekong countries, Lancang-Mekong agricultural cooperation should focus on in-depth cooperation in agricultural technology to extend the industrial chain, promote cooperation among enterprises of all parties and promote agricultural investment and trade exchanges, in order to promote the sustainable development of agriculture in the six Lancang-Mekong countries.

4.1　New Situation and New Challenges

With the support of LMCSF, cooperation and exchanges among Cambodia, China, Laos, Myanmar, Thailand, and Vietnam have been continuously strengthened. Significant results have been achieved in agricultural policy dialogue, industrial upgrading, and capability building. And the projects have made great contributions to regional economy, social development, and people's well-being. However, as the projects progressed, their structure has undergone significant changes, and the field of cooperation has been expanded. In addition, due to the impact of the COVID-19 pandemic, the implementation of future projects will also encounter new challenges.

4.1.1 Expanding Fields of Cooperation

At present, the projects mainly focused on the exchanges and cooperation of agricultural industry technologies, using technical trials, demonstrations, and trainings to enhance the technical level of the agricultural industry development in Lancang-Mekong countries, so as to promote the high-quality development of agriculture. However, with the promotion of technology, the level of agricultural technology in Lancang-Mekong countries has been continuously improved. Based on in-depth cooperation of agricultural technologies, the agricultural cooperation projects should cover the entire agricultural industry chain including multiple aspects of production, processing, trade, etc. Meanwhile, it is necessary to increase cooperation in agricultural capital investment, production management, ecological protection, etc. , to enhance the resilience of Lancang-Mekong agricultural cooperation.

4.1.2 Enhancing Sustainability

At current stage, agricultural production does not take production capacity gaining as the main object. Instead, it is turning to a sustainable development path in which agriculture and natural environment are coordinated. Currently, several Lancang-Mekong agricultural cooperation projects have focused on the co-development of agricultural production and the environment, as well as the sustainable development of aquatic ecology and fisheries. Food security has become an important goal of the Lancang-

Mekong agricultural cooperation projects with the global food system being impacted by the COVID -19 pandemic and natural disasters. Therefore, cooperation in sustainable agricultural development should be strengthened in the future. And the main goal should focus on the coordinated development of agricultural production and the natural environment and regional food security to ensure the sustainable development of agriculture in the Lancang-Mekong region.

4. 1. 3　Hindered International Cooperation and Exchanges

During the COVID -19 pandemic, international cooperation and exchanges are facing new challenges, and the Lancang-Mekong agricultural cooperation projects were no exception. The implementation of the Lancang-Mekong agricultural cooperation project encountered various difficulties. On the one hand, all cross-border movement of people and materials have been blocked. Almost all clustered field activities have been shelved. Technical exchanges and training have been severely affected. On the other hand, international investment and trade have been slow due to the pandemic. Trade costs and barriers have increased, especially the time and expense costs of logistics, warehousing, inspection and quarantine, etc. Thus, the difficulty for countries' trade and investment has increased.

4. 2　New Directions and Measures

After a period of accumulation and summary, Lancang-Mekong agricultural cooperation projects have achieved remarkable results, and gained some experience and practices that can be used for reference. However, we still need to seize new opportunities and use new measures to achieve our goals.

4. 2. 1　New Direction

First, broadening fields of agricultural cooperation. We can further broaden the fields of agricultural cooperation and transit from the agricultural production end to the comprehensive agricultural development to cover multiple fields of processing, sales, etc. Meanwhile, it is necessary to conduct cooperation in integrated industries, such as the combination of "agriculture+leisure tourism".

Second, enhancing cooperation with other departments. By taking into account the weak points of the agricultural development in member countries, we should enhance the cooperation with other fields such as water resources and environment and increase investment in agricultural infrastructure and the supply of supporting services. This will lay a foundation for deepening agricultural cooperation and promoting economic development. Agricultural scientific research institutions of member countries should conduct in-depth cooperation and joint research to develop production technologies, production methods and innovative management models that could specifically fit their local conditions. A long-term cooperation mechanisms and talent exchange training mechanisms for multi-party scientific research institutions should be established.

Third, adding new media for dissemination. It is recommended to establish new media platforms such as the Lancang-Mekong Agricultural Cooperation Project website to improve the multi-channel communication mode such as online, or online and offline combination. Meanwhile, we need to improve the construction of Internet infrastructure in Lancang-Mekong regions to provide new ways and new methods for agricultural cooperation.

Fourth, protecting food security as an important connection. We should actively promote the Lancang-Mekong agricultural cooperation to ensure food security and solve the problems of food supply risk of Lancang-Mekong countries.

4.2.2 New Measures

First, strengthening agricultural policy dialogues. We should put effort on policy dialogue among the agricultural sectors of the six Lancang-Mekong countries, deepen industrial organization cooperation, construct comprehensive legal systems for agricultural investment and cooperation, create an open, inclusive, mutually beneficial and win-win agricultural production capacity cooperation environment; and encourage agricultural policy dialogues between government and enterprises. At the same time, governments of all countries must do a good job in management, guidance and service to ensure fair competition. In addition, leading enterprises should receive preferential treatment in terms of finances, taxes, and policies. Furthermore, we need to enhance traditional friendship, optimizing Lancang-Mekong regional agricultural cooperation system to bring tangible benefits to participating countries and people.

Second, broadening the agricultural industry chain. We should make full use of the comparative advantages of markets and resources of all parties and take the persistence of agricultural cooperation and opening up as the basic direction. It is necessary to further expand the agricultural industry chain and deepen the cooperation and development of the upper, middle and lower reaches of the agricultural industry on the basis of existing cooperation. We must keep enhancing multilateral and bilateral international exchanges and cooperation of agriculture to better serve regional agricultural and rural economic development.

Third, improving agricultural investment and trade. We could make use of international investment and trade to give full play to regional complementary advantages. We could also promote major agricultural product investment and trade promotion activities such as the Agricultural Expo to target differentiated markets in the Lancang-Mekong region. At the same time, we could take this as an opportunity to build a business negotiation platform in the region to promote the continuous expansion of overseas markets for regional specific agro-products. Furthermore, by promoting exchange and cooperation between enterprises, we could increase the influence and visibility of regional specific agro-products, broaden the channels for import and export, and eventually promote the development of agricultural investment and trade.

Fourth, deepening cooperation on agricultural science and technology. By promoting multi-party cooperation, and sharing agricultural cooperation results, regional agricultural could be developed with the support of science and technology. Relying on the supports from scientific research institutes, innovative enterprises and science and technology intermediary organizations, we could establish agricultural technology exchange and cooperation service platforms which could promote agricultural technology exchange and cooperation. Multilateral and bilateral cooperation in various fields such as the utilization and conservation of crop germplasm resources, crop cultivation and breeding technology, and plant protection could be further enhanced. At the same time, we should promote the construction of joint regional agricultural laboratories, demonstration bases, and platforms for production, education and research. By promoting the integration of production, education and research, the development of regional agricultural will be driven by science and technology. In this way, we will create a new pattern of agricultural cooperation in the Lancang-Mekong region and escort the stable implementation of future agricultural cooperation projects.

II

Typical Cases

Chapter 1 | Policy Dialogue

Case 1　Lancang-Mekong Agricultural Cooperation Supporting System Construction Project

1　Objectives

Agriculture is one of the five priority areas of Lancang-Mekong cooperation. Since the launch of the Lancang-Mekong Cooperation 5 years ago, positive progress has been made in multiple areas including agricultural policy dialogue, industrial development, agro-product trade and investment, capacity building and knowledge sharing. In January 2019, the Lancang-Mekong Agricultural Cooperation Center was established, another center under the Lancang-Mekong cooperation mechanism after the Water Resources Cooperation Center, the Environmental Cooperation Center, and the Global Mekong Research Center. The Lancang-Mekong Agricultural Cooperation Center has been carrying out the Lancang-Mekong agricultural cooperation support system construction project for many years. It gave full play to the role of a permanent organization of the Lancang-Mekong Cooperation Joint Working Group on Agriculture and a coordinating organization of regional support to assist the operation of the Lancang-Mekong agricultural cooperation mechanism. The center has carried out the research on planning of the Lancang-Mekong agricultural cooperation, helped planning and promoting the implementation of the LMC Bumper Harvest projects. A supporting service system of the Lancang-Mekong agricultural cooperation has been established to support the stable development of Lancang-Mekong agricultural cooperation in terms of mechanism improvement, project implementation, and research planning.

2 Activities

2. 1 Mechanism Meeting of the Lancang-Mekong Cooperation Joint Working Group on Agriculture（LMC-JWGA）

In September 2017，the LMC-JWGA was formally established and operated in an orderly manner. Member countries took turns to host annual working group meetings. In June 2019，the second meeting of LMC-JWGA was held in Siem Reap，Cambodia. The heads of delegations from Cambodia and China jointly served as the chairperson of the meeting. In October 2020，the third meeting of LMC-JWGA was held online.

2. 2 Establishment of Lancang-Mekong Agricultural Cooperation Supporting Organization

In January 2019，the Lancang-Mekong Agricultural Cooperation Center（LMAC）was officially established under Foreign Economic Cooperation Center（FECC）of the Ministry of Agriculture and Rural Affairs（MARA）of China. In August 2019，the Lancang-Mekong Cooperation Agricultural Science and Technology Exchange and Cooperation Group was established. In June 2020，Guangxi Branch of Lancang-Mekong Agricultural Cooperation Center was established.

2. 3 Lancang-Mekong Agricultural Cooperation Planning Research

In January 2020，the *Three-Year Plan of Action on Lancang-Mekong Agricultural Cooperation* (*2020-2022*) organized and drafted by LMAC was formally approved during the Fifth Lancang-Mekong Cooperation Foreign Ministers' Meeting and became the first guiding document in agricultural field of Lancang-Mekong cooperation. LMAC began to organize the compilation of *Lancang-Mekong Agricultural Cooperation Development Report* in 2019. The report regularly summarizes the progress，effectiveness，experience and practices of Lancang-Mekong agricultural cooperation for the exchange and learning between agricultural

departments and related institutions in the six Lancang-Mekong countries. At the end of March 2021, the first report was officially published in China Agriculture Press in both Chinese and English.

2.4 Management of the Lancang-Mekong Agricultural Cooperation Projects

LMAC assisted the application and implementation of China's projects under the Lancang-Mekong Cooperation Special Fund. It regularly tracked the progress of the project, and promptly put forward relevant suggestions to promote the in-depth development of the project. Meanwhile, LMAC have explored solutions to problems such as small scale of agricultural projects, scattered fields, insufficient coordination, and weak continuity. LMAC proposed the LMC Bumper Harvest projects which was recognized and adopted.

2.5 The First Sub-regional Online Agricultural Technology Promotion and Information Exchange Platform

Various agricultural scientific and technological resources and market information were integrated in the newly constructed Lancang-Mekong Agricultural Extension and Information Platform (mobile App) to promote the sharing of agricultural technology and agricultural information in Lancang-Mekong region. The platform exports China's advanced practical agricultural technology and agricultural information service models to innovate agricultural information service in Mekong countries, enhances the exchange of agricultural policies, information sharing and achievement transformation in the Lancang-Mekong region.

3 Achievements

3.1 Improving Lancang-Mekong Agricultural Cooperation Mechanism and Constructing a Sub-regional Agricultural Coordination and Linkage System

The LMC-JWGA has been playing an active role in promoting policy communication, strategy alignment, and cooperation and coordination among Lancang-Mekong countries. It has led the maintenance and construction of sub-regional agricultural cooperation mechanisms. LMAC was successfully established to be the permanent executive agency of the LMC-JWGA. The center fulfilled the function of a regional supporting service organization and promoted the global development of LMAC. The center also actively implemented the proposal of "promoting sharing and cooperation in the field of agricultural science and technology, supporting information sharing and exchanges among scientific research institutions as well as mutual personnel visiting" in the *Five-Year Plan of Action on Lancang-Mekong Cooperation* (2018-2022). What's more, it promoted the establishment of the Exchange and Cooperation Consortium for Agricultural Science and Technology in the Lancang-Mekong Cooperation (ECCAST-LMC) to improve the cooperation platform mechanism, which has laid an important foundation for scientific and technological exchanges and cooperation in the fields of planting, animal husbandry, and fishery. Relying on the geographical advantages of Guangxi-ASEAN agricultural cooperation, LMAC promoted the establishment of the Guangxi Branch of Lancang-Mekong Agricultural Cooperation Center which facilitated the exchange and cooperation of agricultural science and technology, economy and trade, and talents in Lancang-Mekong sub-region. The establishment of the Lancang-Mekong Agricultural Cooperation Industry Cooperation Group, the Lancang-Mekong Animal Veterinary Medicine Vaccine Industry Alliance, and the Lancang-Mekong Agricultural Cooperation Information Exchange Group are being prepared in an orderly manner. A supporting system with multi-cooperation team, collaborating group, and platform cooperation has gradually formed, which plays vital roles in technical support, multi-party coordination, and information sharing.

3. 2　Promoting the Research on the Planning of Lancang-Mekong Cooperation and the Sharing of Knowledge and Information

The *Three-Rear Action Plan for Lancang-Mekong Agricultural Cooperation* (*2020-2022*) was drafted and formally approved during the Fifth LMC Foreign Ministers' Meeting, and listed as one of the achievements of the Third LMC Leaders' Meeting. The plan relied on the coordination and support from LMAC to focus on priority cooperation areas such as agricultural cooperation policy dialogue, industrial revitalization, and trade development, which played a guiding role in strategy alignment and project implementation of Lancang-Mekong agricultural cooperation. LMAC kept on tracking and summarized the progress, effectiveness and experience of the sub-regional Lancang-Mekong agricultural cooperation, and edited them into the *Report on the Development of Lancang-Mekong Agricultural Cooperation*, which has been published formally. The report provided a pragmatic reference for the Lancang-Mekong Cooperation Agricultural Joint Working Group as well as other relevant departments and scientific research institutions of member countries, which has promoted the all-round improvement and upgrading of agricultural cooperation. LMAC has also carried out basic research on agriculture in local provinces and regions to promote cooperation with scientific research institutions, project implementation units and enterprises. The innovative development of key industries such as rice and tropical cash crops has been promoted, which has improved the continuous deepening of cooperation in the quality and safety of agro-products. The comprehensive competitiveness of sub-regional agriculture was enhanced correspondingly.

3. 3　Assisting the Planning of Lancang-Mekong Agricultural Projects and Improving the Quality and Efficiency of Agricultural Cooperation

By focusing on advantageous agricultural industries such as farming, animal husbandry and fishery, LMAC assisted the application and implementation of Asian cooperation funds. It also promoted cooperation in various aspects such as platform construction, joint research, experiment and demonstration, and capability building, which have promoted the optimization and upgrading of the agricultural industrial chain and value chain in Lancang-Mekong sub-region. It put efforts to implement the initiative of LMC Bumper Harvest projects that Premier Li Keqiang proposed during the Third LMC Leaders' Meeting. By combining the characteristics of agricultural development in various countries in terms of policy dialogue, industrial development, investment and trade, and capability building, LMAC focused on key areas and industries and promoted a batch of high-quality projects, which have made great contribution to the construction of the Lancang-Mekong River economic development belt.

4 Impacts

4.1 Improved Lancang-Mekong Agricultural Cooperation Mechanism

The LMC-JWGA operates efficiently. As the fourth center under the Lancang-Mekong cooperation mechanism, LMAC is playing the role as a regional supporting service organization.

4.2 A platform for Agricultural and Rural Policy Communication, Experience Exchange and Economic and Trade

By holding of the Lancang-Mekong Agricultural and Rural Development Cooperation Forum and operating the model operation of Lancang-Mekong Agricultural Extension and Information Platform, the collaboration and exchanges between multiple parties have been continuously improved.

4.3 Project Connections and Cooperation on Key Industries

By assisting in the overall management of Lancang-Mekong agricultural cooperation projects, LMAC focused on key industrial areas and promoted project connections and cooperation, which led to the development of

regional key industries and cooperation.

5 Difficulties and Challenges

The construction of the Lancang-Mekong agricultural cooperation system and the progress of liaison and exchange work have been affected by COVID-19 pandemic to a certain extent. The cross-border movement of people was blocked. Activities were difficult to carry out normally. The progress of project was relatively slow. The promotion of the Lancang-Mekong Agricultural Extension and Information Platform in Mekong countries has been affected.

6 Successful Experiences

6.1 Innovation and Enhancement of Mechanism System Construction and Maintenance

It is necessary to make full use of the existing platforms such as Guangxi Branch of Lancang-Mekong Agricultural Cooperation, Lancang-Mekong Cooperation Agricultural Science and Technology Exchange and Cooperation Group, as well as local advantages, to maintain contacts with multinational enterprises and relevant institutions in Mekong countries to jointly promote work.

6.2 Integration and Key Project Promotions and Brand Construction

It is necessary to integrate project resources to improve project database construction. We must deeply understand and explore the demands of the agro-product markets of Lancang-Mekong countries, so that we could focus on key areas and promote project implementations. Meanwhile, we should try to win the support from the Mekong countries to promote the orderly development of the LMC Bumper Harvest projects. And then, we have to put forward a list of projects around key topics. Lastly, we must improve the project database and expert database, and establish projects as brands.

6.3 Publicity and Collection of and Research on Basic Information in Lancang-Mekong Agricultural Cooperation

It is necessary to strengthen publicity and regularly review the progress, research results, and the effectiveness of key projects of Lancang-Mekong agricultural cooperation. Achievements should be promoted through various channels such as media, conferences, and forums. We must assure the collection of information and research on each country and key industries of Mekong countries. By improving technical support and policy suggestion capabilities, we can lay a solid foundation for the improvement of the mechanism system and the establishment of the projects as brands.

Case 2   A Lancang-Mekong Comprehensive Agricultural Cooperation Project Using TV Programs as the Medium

1   Objectives

The media is considered a window of understanding, a bond of friendship, and a bridge for cooperation. The Lancang-Mekong cooperation mechanism has established three pillars of political security, sustainable economic development, and society and humanities. Media cooperation is an important part of social and humanistic cooperation.

Relying on TV programs, the Lancang-Mekong Regional Comprehensive Agricultural Cooperation Project aims to enhance media cooperation between Lancang-Mekong countries, increase the spread of Lancang-Mekong pragmatic cooperation, and enhance mutual understanding and trust between all six countries. Improving novel methods for media exchanges and cooperation, building a bridge of people-to-people bonds and enhancing public support for Lancang-Mekong cooperation would contribute to the building of a community of shared future among Lancang-Mekong countries.

2   Activities

In response to the Lancang-Mekong Cooperation initiative and promote the continuous development of Lancang-Mekong agricultural cooperation, the China Agricultural Film and TV Center was successfully granted for the Lancang-Mekong Cooperation Special Fund and produced 60 episodes of *China Farm* in October 2019. It mainly covered contents such as science and technology and rich experience, which has improved the exchanges of agricultural and rural cultural among Lancang-Mekong countries.

The project team sent a number of film crews to the Mekong River

Basin countries to film and produce 32 new episodes of *China Farm*. Among them, 17 episodes were science and technology programs describing the planting and breeding technology, industrial development experience and advanced concepts suitable for the agricultural characteristics in the Mekong countries. The show covered multiple topics including coconut, cassava, fall armyworm, dragon fruit, coffee, cocoa, agarwood, sugar cane, rubber, pepper, edible fungus, cantaloupe, etc., such as the episodes of *Fruitful Development of Cassava* and *Joint Fight Against Fall Armyworm*. 13 episodes were about bilateral cooperation, introducing the story of Chinese entrepreneurs collaborating with farmers in the Mekong countries to start businesses, and the stories about mutual and heart-to-heart connection among the peoples of the Lancang-Mekong countries, such as the episodes of *Joining Hands to Raise Delicious Food*, *Chinese Who Started Businesses in Vietnam Alone*, and *Deeper and Broader China-Thailand Agricultural Cooperation*. 2 episodes were about joint fight against poverty, showing the Chinese government's poverty alleviation work in the Mekong River Basin countries, such as the episodes of *China-Myanmar Cooperation to Fight Poverty* and *China-Cambodia Family*. The program extolled the profound friendship between the six Lancang-Mekong countries by presenting the characters' inner feelings, career development, and humanistic care. Apart from being released on domestic new media platforms such as Nongshi. com, the reproduced and new programs were also broadcasted on mainstream media in the Mekong countries to conduct an all-media matrix propagation in the Lancang-Mekong region.

3　Achievements

3.1　Enhancing the Spread of Agricultural and Rural Culture

China Farm was the first regular thematic TV column sharing China's agricultural science and technology and rich experience that was on air in

Mekong countries. By telling stories of agriculture and spreading the wisdom of farmers, the column not only drew attentions of urban audience in the Mekong countries on agriculture, but also directly connected local farmer audience and shared practical farming techniques with them. This program has promoted connections between cultures, agricultures, and people among countries in the Mekong sub-region. In addition, the program has further deepened the cooperation and friendship among the six Lancang-Mekong countries.

3.2 Promoting the Exchange and Sharing of Agricultural Technology

Agriculture occupies an important position in the economic development of all Lancang-Mekong countries. The Mekong countries have unique conditions for the development of agriculture such as fertile soil, excellent climatic conditions, and a large agricultural population. Meanwhile, they also have an urgent need for advanced technology to rapidly develop agriculture. The translated versions of *China Farm* for Mekong countries upheld the professionalism, service, and practicality that agricultural programs have always pursued. Through regular weekly broadcasts throughout the year in the mainstream media of the Mekong countries, China's advanced agricultural technology of planting and breeding, as well as rich experience and concepts were truly shared with local farmers. It helped local farmers to improve production skills, average output, and farming efficiency gradually, which led to higher yields and better life.

3.3 Deepening the Communication and Connection Between the Media

The Lancang-Mekong cooperation mechanism has shown vigor and vitality since the launch. It has become a "golden brand" for building an Asian community of shared future. As a business card to showcase China's domestic-foreign communication of agriculture, *China Farm* has worked with mainstream media from the Mekong countries to promote the main theme of good-neighbor and friendship, as well as the new achievement of win-win cooperation, resulting in a positive public opinion atmosphere that supports the promotion of Lancang-Mekong cooperation. It has played an important and irreplaceable role in escorting the stable and sustainable development of the Lancang-Mekong cooperation.

4 Impacts

TV programs such as *China Farm* went deep into the field of cooperative partner countries. By establishing an effective communication system for sharing experience, knowledge and information with other countries, the project has improved welfare of the local people, and effectively enhanced the cooperation and friendship between the mainstream media of the Lancang-Mekong basin countries. By integrating resources effectively, the project has improved the sustainable communication capability with regional demonstration effect. The programs were broadcasted through local mainstream TV channels. Thus, it could broadly benefit the local families. By broadcasting in local official languages, the programs were effectively listened and learned by local people, which has effectively improved the visibility and the credibility of the program. In addition to the function of cultural communication, it was more important for the program to call on people to know about the scientific and technological development results achieved by the Lancang-Mekong agricultural cooperation, and encourage people to apply them after they watched the program.

5 Difficulties and Challenges

5.1 Unclear Viewing Data of the Program Broadcast

Since most of the Mekong countries lack market research companies that professionally analyze TV ratings and do not have the ability to gain insight into the market performance of the programs. *China Farm* TV

Program has difficulties in receiving intuitive digital feedback after it is broadcast. Program broadcast and satisfaction feedback mainly come from feedback from local TV stations and embassies. In the absence of viewing data, it is hard to improve and promote the column.

5. 2 Unstable Broadcast of the Program

According to the preliminary investigation of mainstream TV channels in the Mekong countries, there were uncontrollable elements over the schedule of *China Farm*. For example, the scheduled broadcast can be cancelled due to holidays and other issues, which restricted the broadcast of the program.

6 Successful Experiences

6. 1 Strict Control Over All Aspects of Program Production

According to the actual implementation of this project, the theme of the program has been matched by all aspects including the overall title of the column, the clips, the selection of the host and the costumes, the studio setting, etc. All of above should highlight the local customs of Mekong countries. Therefore, the program can be more suitable for the appetite of the local audience in the Mekong countries, and the ultimate effect of the practicality of the program can be achieved.

6. 2 Accurate Program Topic Selection

The topic selection of the program must not only meet the agricultural characteristics and the needs of the Mekong countries, but also cover the agriculture-related hot topics that are most concerned by the Mekong countries nowadays. For example, the topic of fall armyworm was selected since it was an agricultural security issue that many Asian countries were facing and paying close attention to in 2019.

6. 3 Strict Quality Control of the Program

After strict review and quality control, in order to better control the political standards and ensure that the program content and production level meet the quality standards and related policies of external communication，the project invited a number of experts to review all the programs. The production team edited and improved the program based on expert advice，and finally completed the production of *China Farm*.

6.4 Professional Translation

Yunnan Radio and Television Station International Channel，a partner of the project，has gathered a group of translators of Southeast Asia and South Asia minor languages over the years relying on its unique geographic advantages. In addition，it is also backed up by a group of translators mainly composed of announcers from national TV channels of the Mekong countries，which has laid a solid foundation for the translation of *China Farm*.

6.5 Multi-platform Broadcasting

In order to promote the overall influence of the project in all Lancang-Mekong countries，the Chinese version of *China Farm* was broadcasted on domestic new media platforms such as Nongshi. com. The translated versions of the program were broadcasted on the mainstream media channels of Mekong countries that partnering with China Agricultural Film and TV Center，such as Laos National TV，Cambodian Commercial TV，Myanmar Skynet TV，and Lancang-Mekong TV.

Chapter 2 | Industrial Development and Promotion

Case 3　Myanmar Coffee Production and Quality Improvement Project

Myanmar is located in the tropics, with a warm and rainy climate and fertile soil. Thus, Myanmar is an excellent coffee planting area. The coffee industry could be one of the most promising areas of agricultural development in Myanmar. In order to establish an effective connection with the global market, the Myanmar government is encouraging the expansion of coffee planting area. However, the improvement of coffee production and quality have been seriously hindered due to many shortcomings in planting techniques, processing techniques, and machinery and equipment. As a result, Myanmar urgently needs project funding support. In this context, Ministry of Agriculture, Livestock and Irrigation of Myanmar has implemented the Coffee Production and Quality Improvement Project with the support of the Lancang-Mekong Cooperation Special Fund.

1　Objectives

Concerning the upgrading of coffee production and quality, the project has four main objectives: to explore innovative coffee planting techniques, improve farmers' planting skills, and increase coffee production in Myanmar; to improve the income and livelihood of Myanmar farmers; to improve the quality of coffee and enhance its export competitiveness to form competitive advantages of the coffee industry in international trade; to improve the management skills of Myanmar farmers, assist them transform from producers to operators, and enhance the comprehensive coffee production capacity.

2　Activities

2.1　Training of Coffee Planting and Processing

During this coffee production and quality improvement projects, 14 specialty coffee production trainings with a total of 1,639 trainees were conducted in Myanmar's Chin State, Kachin State, Shan State, Mandalay Division, and Magway Division. In addition, a total 2 times of the Trainings of Trainers (TOT) was conducted to 97 trainees in Bago and Mandalay Divisions successfully.

2.2 Investigation and Learning

In order to learn the cutting-edge technology and mature experience of coffee planting and management, six staffs from the Ministry of Agriculture, Livestock and Irrigation of Myanmar were dispatched to Vietnam to learn Robusta coffee planting and processing technology on August 21 to 24, 2019. After that, on June 29, 2020, the farmers from Chin State of Myanmar were organized to visit the Coffee Research, Information, Extension and Training Center in Pyin Oo Lwin City, Mandalay Division. Moreover, farmers from Nat Yay Kan Village, Magway Division were organized to visit the Coffee Technology Development Farm to particularly learn coffee planting and processing technology on November 7, 2020.

2.3 Myanmar Coffee Forum 2019

The "Myanmar Coffee Forum 2019" was successfully held at Mercure Mandalay Hill Resort Hotel, Mandalay Region on May 15th, 2019 with a total of 365 attendees (Fig. 1). The forum focused on coffee planting in Myanmar and the development of related industries, the international frontier issues of coffee production and processing technology, and summarized the difficulties and challenges faced at the current stage. The coffee forum has gathered contacts for the development of the coffee industry, and played a very important role in publicity and promotion at the same time.

2.4 Standardized Coffee Production Services

In order to standardized coffee planting and quality control, various

Fig. 1　Myanmar Coffee Forum 2019

standardized coffee production services were provided to the project area, including the distribution of coffee seeds, seedlings, and pamphlets (Fig. 2). A total of 109 kilograms of seeds, 256,800 plants of seedlings, and 20,000 shade trees were distributed. In addition, a number of pamphlets that introduces modern coffee planting methods and technologies have been issued to growers to promote the standardization of coffee production.

Fig. 2　Coffee Seeds and Pamphlets

2.5　Coffee Planting and Processing Machines and Equipments

The project mainly provided coffee drying trays and pulping machines. Among them, there are 16 drying trays (Fig. 3) and 12 sets of pulping machines. The project also provided practical tools such as augers, coffee refractometers, pruning scissors, pruning saws and grafting knives to coffee clusters in Myanmar. At the same time, in order to promote coffee quality research and improvement, the project also purchased coffee processing facilities including one set of laboratory equipment, one pulping machine, one sizing machine, one coffee roaster (Fig. 4) and one set of coffee cup quality evaluation equipment.

Fig. 3　Coffee Drying Trays　　　　　　Fig. 4　Coffee Roaster

3　Achievements

3.1　Significantly Improved Coffee Production Technology

We have launched coffee production trainings which covered topics including seed selection and seedling, germination and planting, field management, and harvesting and processing. Thus, the farmers in Myanmar have mastered scientific planting and processing technology, and coffee production have been standardized gradually. In addition, farmers have continuously broadened their horizons, their willingness and enthusiasm to learn and accept new production technologies during the excursion to abroad. More than 1,600 people participated in the training courses, and the exchange and learning among farmers produced a great spillover effect, expanding the scope of popularization of production technologies, and making more groups benefit from the training activities. In the process, the coffee production technology has been improved.

3.2 Greatly Enhanced the Output and Quality of Coffee

During the trainings and excursions, the planting and processing of coffee in Myanmar has been standardized gradually. The yield per unit has been significantly increased, as well as the total output. In addition, the production process of coffee products has been more sophisticated with the use of machinery and equipment such as drying trays, pulping machines, and roasters. The quality has been significantly improved. It now matches the international level. Thus, the competitiveness of Myanmar coffee in international market has increased.

3.3 Fairly Raised the Income and Livelihood of Myanmar Farmers

The Improvement of Coffee Production and Quality Project received financial support from the Myanmar government. In 2018-2019 fiscal year, the government provided a budget of US $ 117,000 and in 2019—2020 fiscal year US $ 64,000. With this support, the coffee industry has developed rapidly. The output and quality have been significantly improved. In particular, the output of high-quality coffee has increased rapidly, which has successfully integrated with the international market with a clear price advantage. The increased output and low price have brought positive effect. The income and the livelihood of the coffee growers in Myanmar have been significantly improved.

4 Impacts

4. 1 Remarkable Project Results

The expected goal is to implement this project in 3 places in Myanmar, carry out 4 specialty coffee production trainings, train about 250 trainees, and hold 1 TOT. While the actual result far exceeded expectations. The project implemented area expanded to 6 places; it actually launched 14 specialty coffee production trainings with 1,639 trainees, and 2 TOT with 97 trainees. The project has been effectively implemented, and farmers in the project area are able to use modern technology to produce high-quality and specialty coffee which brings fruitful economic effects.

4. 2 Great Potential of the Project

With the support from Lancang-Mekong Cooperation Special Fund, Myanmar Coffee Production and Quality Improvement Project has progressed smoothly and has achieved remarkable results. Until now, a total of more than 1,600 coffee growers participated in the trainings, and 97 participated in TOT. With the assistance from China, Myanmar has gradually established a coffee industry. The coffee industry has become more and more stable under the support of relevant measures, which has formed a growth pole for the coffee industry with huge development potential. At the same time, the smooth implementation of the project has deepen the China-Myanmar bilateral cooperation with better communication and lasting friendship.

5 Difficulties and Challenges

5. 1 Funding Gap in Implementing the Project

On the one hand, there is an issue of depreciation of project funds due to the unstable exchange rate. On the other hand, the supply of funding is not timely enough. Especially during the COVID-19 pandemic, the project budget has not been revised on time, resulting in a gap in funding which affected the project progress.

5. 2 Lack of Trained Personnel in Technology Research and Development

In order to improve the quality of coffee, the project provided a large number of experimental equipments for related research. However, there is a shortage of personnel engaging in experiment and research, and most participants were not familiar with the operation and application of laboratory equipments, resulting in limitations in improving coffee quality.

6 Experiences

6. 1 Aiming at Competitive Industries and Stimulating Industrial Potential

Myanmar has natural advantages of growing high-quality coffee from the perspectives of altitude, temperature, rainfall, water supply, soil and slope. However, due to the limited basic conditions of Myanmar, the coffee industry has been well developed, the industrial advantages has not been well exploited, and economic development lacks pillar industries as driving forces. Relying on the Lancang-Mekong Cooperation Special Fund, China provides special financial support to Myanmar to develop the coffee industry. Myanmar's coffee industry has shown a rapid development trend with the support of external funds, and the project's effectiveness matches the expectation.

6. 2 Targeting a Single Field and Providing Supporting Facilities

Myanmar Coffee Production and Quality Improvement mainly focused on one field the coffee production, and provided pre-and mid-production supporting facilities and services including high-quality seedlings, production trainings, excursions to aboard, mechanical equipments and laboratory equipments. As a result of the project strategy of "concentrating strength and making comprehensive breakthroughs", the coffee industry in Myanmar has

accomplished leapfrog development with improvement in terms of both the production and quality, and farmers' income and livelihood have been significantly improved correspondingly.

Case 4　Myanmar Rural Development and Vegetable Cultivation Technology Transfer Project

As a major producer of vegetable, Myanmar has the potential to become a major global vegetable exporter. However, vegetable farming is a knowledge intensive subsector of agriculture. It requires professional knowledge and labor input. Since vegetable farmers produce a variety of vegetable species in relatively short production cycles, this process requires a wide range of knowledge, skills and information. Whereas most farmers in the project areas lack vegetable planting techniques and knowledge of vegetable management and protection. In addition, due to the increasing price of agricultural inputs, vegetable planting costs have been at a high level, and the benefits of planting vegetables have been low. Therefore, in order to cultivate Myanmar's vegetable industry and develop the socioeconomic status of the target rural areas, it is necessary to provide vegetable farmers with basic knowledge and information on vegetable planting, and try to use them in the fields. Under this context, the Ministry of Agriculture, Livestock and Irrigation of Myanmar has implemented Myanmar Rural Development and Vegetable Cultivation Technology Transfer Project.

1　Objects

This project focuses on the following five aspects. First, to improve the agricultural productivity, increase farmers' income, and improve their quality of life by developing vegetable industry. Second, to strengthen the capability of farmers, vegetable producers and processing groups by exchanging and transferring knowledge, technology and experience on vegetable cultivation. Third, to provide staff capacity building on vegetable cultivation technology so as to strengthen the support of trained

130

personnel for Myanmar agriculture. Fourth, to create the vegetable training program, establish long-term training mechanism and build Myanmar farmer expert teams so as to raise awareness of vegetable cultivation technology. Fifth, to establish the working vegetable demonstration farms that will showcase new ideas and techniques and serve as an educational community center.

2 Activities

2.1 Baseline Data Survey

More than 200 farmers from 10 main vegetable growing areas were selected for baseline survey at the initial stage of project (Fig. 1). The strength and weakness of vegetable cultivation technology at the current stage are analyzed based on the survey data. Based on the results of baseline survey, the required knowledge and information has been tailored by the project expert team to fulfill the practical needs of the farmers in such a way that the information contributed by the project can be useful in resolving their challenges.

Fig. 1 Baseline Data Survey

2.2 Training of Vegetable Cultivation Technology

The Myanmar Vegetable and Fruit Research and Development Center (VFRDC) arranged the training of vegetable cultivation management for farmers and also prepared the training manuals (Fig. 2). Firstly, it organized the TOT training for 50 DOA staffs from project areas who have background experiences on vegetable production. Secondly, farmer trainings were individually conducted at 9 villages in Yangon Division, Bago Division and Ayeyarwaddy Division and totally 450 farmers attended the trainings. The training duration was one week. The following subjects were provided in the training manuals: vegetable cultivation guides, soil nutrient management, vegetable seed production, hybrid seed production, soil fertility evaluation (theory + practical), making natural fertilizers and pesticides (theory + practical), vermiculture and vermicomposting (theory + practical), organic agriculture (theory + practical), GAP vegetable production (theory + practical), postharvest management on vegetables, year-round vegetable production, vegetable off-season production against climate-change, home gardening, disease and pest prevention and management, protective cultivation technology, management and storage technology of vegetable seeds.

Fig. 2   Training of Cultivation Technology

2.3   Establishment of Demonstration Farms and Conducting Farmer Field Day

The project team has established demonstration farms in Yangon Division, Bago Division and Ayeyarwaddy Division and used them as agricultural teaching center to carry out farmer field day activities

(Fig. 3). The project supported the agricultural inputs such as vegetable seeds, fertilizers, pesticides, tools, backpack sprayer, etc., and vegetable technical support pre- and mid-production to the pilot farmers. At the same time, different kinds of vegetables were grown in their fields under the supervision of vegetable expert team and regional DOA staffs. Then, the farmers and observers from the related areas were invited to explore the cultivation technology of vegetables at the project demonstration farms.

Fig. 3　Demonstration Farms and Farmer Field Day Activity

2.4　Technical Exchanges Among Lancang-Mekong Region Countries

The project team went to Vietnam and carried out a 7-day vegetable cultivation technology exchange activity (Fig. 4). 10 experts participated in this exchange activity, visiting the Vegetable Research Institute, Hanoi and top vegetable producers in Hanoi, Danan and Halong. In addition, the experts also visited the Institute of Agricultural Science of Southern Vietnam, Hochi Min Potato Research Center, and the vegetable growing areas in southern Vietnam. They particularly focused on issues such as vegetable market information, cultivation techniques (hydroponics and aerobics systems), and food security.

Fig. 4　Vegetable Technical Exchanges Among Lancang-Mekong Region Countries

3　Achievements

The project has been implemented effectively and achieved fruitful results in the following four aspects.

3. 1　The Baseline Data Survey

At the initial stage of the project, the project team first collected soil and water samples from 10 project areas and tested nutrient content, organic matter content, mineral content, and biological indicators to evaluate whether the investigated area is suitable for vegetable cultivation and formed a systematic evaluation report.

3. 2　Vegetable Demonstration Farm

This project established demonstration farms in 10 regions and launched several farmer field day activities. These has formed a strong radiating effect and benefited a large number of vegetable growers.

3. 3　Vegetable Cultivation Training

The project has carried out vegetable cultivation training workshops in 4 regions, with more than 240 trainees. At the same time, a total of 10 people participated in the technical visit to Vietnam and composed a research report and video report.

3. 4　Income from Vegetable Planting

During this project, the income of vegetable growers increased significantly. According to survey data, the growth of net cash income per acre of every vegetable production from 2019 to 2020 was between 7.2% ~ 21.2%, whereas eggplant showed the highest rate of change of 21.2% in average (Fab. 1).

Tab. 1　Average Net Cash Income (NCI) for Vegetable
Production Per Acre from 2019 to 2020

Unit: MMKs/acre, %

Crop	Average NCI in 2019	Average NCI in 2020	Change in average NCI from 2019 to 2020
Eggplant	540,000	654,480	21. 2
Yard Long Bean	350,000	396,900	13. 4
Okra	565,000	662,745	17. 3
Radish	230,000	246,560	7. 2
Green Chili	265,000	316,675	19. 5
Sweet Corn	375,000	408,000	8. 8
Average	387,500	447,560	15. 5

Taken together, the project has achieved remarkable results, and the vegetable industry has shown a leap-forward development trend.

4　Impacts

4. 1　Effectively Promoted Green Agriculture in Myanmar

Myanmar vegetable farmers have changed significantly in terms of both mentality and skills during the project, which is reflected in the increased confidence in vegetable planting and the significant improvement in knowledge and technology. Especially after participating in the project training, Myanmar vegetable farmers showed a keen interest in the application of organic agricultural technology in the vegetable field. Specifically, vegetable farmers can make biofertilizers and organic input elements such as EM Bokashi compost, vermiculture & vermicompost, natural foliar fertilizer & pesticide, Fermented Fruit Juice, Fish Amino Acid, etc. Most farmers have a deep understanding of green agriculture through the project, and people have begun to pay attention to the sustainability of agriculture, and can reduce the input of pesticides, fertilizers and other chemicals in practice. As a result, green agriculture has been practically developed.

4.2 Extremely High Satisfaction on the Project Implementation

In September 2020, the result of a survey of satisfaction degree on project implementation was analyzed. First, 12 trained vegetable farmers from Yangon Division, Bago Division and Ayeyarwaddy Division participated the survey. Data showed that these vegetable farmers were quite satisfied with the project. Among them, 16% rated 100 points, 40% rated 80 points, 43% rated 60 points, and no one expressed dissatisfaction. The project has basically achieved the expected goals. This project benefited participants, greatly promoted the regional economic development and won the high recognition of Myanmar vegetable farmers.

4.3 Further Deepened China-Myanmar Cooperation

Myanmar Rural Development and Vegetable Cultivation Technology Transfer Project is one of the key projects of the Lancang-Mekong Cooperation Special Fund. Through this project, both China and Myanmar are able to develop in cooperation and realize the importance of bilateral cooperation. Relying on this, China and Myanmar will carry out broader and deeper cooperation to actively create opportunities for assistance and connections, and promote regional economic integration.

5 Difficulties and Challenges

5.1 Low Training Efficiency

Most farmers in the project areas have mainly followed traditional cultivation techniques. It was not easy for them to accept the concept of using new technologies and new methods. Thus, the training efficiency was low and short-term result was insignificant. In addition, most farmers in the project areas had no direct access knowledge bases like institutes, literature, Internet and mobile networks. In many cases, farmers are illiterate. Thus, they lacked the knowledge of new technologies, concepts, and methods. The theories delivered by vegetable cultivation technology training and various workshops were difficult for them to digest.

5.2 Not Yet Achieved the Leading Role

At present, the benefited group was mainly the project participants. Judging from the result, the project was implemented in limited areas with a small number of participants. Meanwhile, the project was not well publicized. Taken together, only a small group of people benefited from the project, and its potential spillover effect was not effectively tapped and brought into play.

6 Experiences

6.1 Baseline Survey

In the early stage of the project, the soil and water samples in the project areas were tested for nutrient content, organic matter content, mineral content, and biological indicators, which allowed us to perform a scientific evaluation of the adaptability of vegetable planting. These works laid an important foundation for the smooth development of the following stages of the project. In fact, the strength of agriculture is mainly affected by resource endowments such as climate, soil and water. Therefore, it is indispensable to conduct necessary resource condition testing before implementing agricultural projects to ensure a targeted project and avoid unnecessary losses.

6. 2　Establishment of Demonstration Farms

Several vegetable demonstration farms were established in Yangon Division, Bago Division and Ayeyarwaddy Division during the project. Recourses such as seeds, fertilizers, pesticides, sprayers, and pruning tools were provided to these farms to promote the development of demonstration farms. These vegetable demonstration farms were built as successful models to play a strong demonstration and leading role, and provide development guidelines for other farms. Also, we concentrated limited resources such as funds, talents, and technology to ensure the establishment of demonstration farms. And then, these farms can lead other farms to develop. This can also make use of the advantages of latecomers and increase the overall development speed with the.

6. 3　Timely Adjustment of the Strategy in Response to Feedbacks

The effectiveness of project implementation needs to be evaluated by investigation and assessment after the project. A satisfaction survey was conducted on participants in Yangon Division, Bago Division and Ayeyarwaddy Division in the later stage of the project and analyzed. In this way, we can better evaluate the real effects of project and answer the questions such as whether it benefited farmers, whether it promoted rural economic development, and whether the expected goals were achieved. At the same time, the implementation strategy can be adjusted in time according to possible shortcomings.

Case 5   Lancang-Mekong Sub-regional Rice Green Yield-increasing Technology Experiment and Demonstration Project

Lancang-Mekong Sub-regional Rice Green Yield-increasing Technology Experiment and Demonstration Project, a key project of the Lancang-Mekong agricultural cooperation in planting industry, is organized jointly by Guangxi Agricultural Vocational College with several multinational agricultural enterprises, to carried out experiments and demonstrations of rice green yield-increasing technology and experiments of rice field comprehensive planting model in Cambodia, Myanmar, Laos, and Vietnam, with the aim of increasing rice green yield-increasing application technology in the Lancang-Mekong sub-region and promoting green, high-quality, and efficient development of regional rice industry.

1   Objectives

Based on the regional advantages of Guangxi and ASEAN countries, such as similar climate and geographical proximity, as well as the green rice production increase technology and model developed by Guangxi that is suitable for low-latitude regions, 4 experimental stations for Superior Crop Varieties have been built in Cambodia, Myanmar, Laos, and Vietnam. These stations were used as a platform for technical exchange and promotion to demonstrate and promote green rice yield-increasing technologies and models suitable for the region. On the one hand, this project can promote the food production in the Lancang-Mekong region to achieve the goals of green, high-yield, high-quality, and high-efficiency, and to ensure regional food security; on the other hand, this project can enhance the income of local farmers and promote the sustainable development of agriculture through training and technical assistance to farmers in Lancang-Mekong regions.

139

2 Activities

This project carried out activities such as introduction and demonstration of new rice varieties, improvement of rice green yield-increasing technology, experiments of comprehensive rice planting and breeding models, personnel training, demonstration, promotion and optimization and organization of suitable green rice yield-increasing technologies. Details are as the following:

2.1 Establishment of Rice Green Yield-increasing Technology Experiment and Demonstration Bases

Through the establishment of rice green yield-increasing technology experiment and demonstration bases, technical experiments and demonstrations such as planting, raising seedlings, water and fertilizer management, and disease and pest prevention and management were carried out to main rice varieties (Fig. 1). Up to now, this project has established a total of 8,655 mu of experiment and demonstration bases and driven an area of more than 44,030 mu land to use the same technologies. Among them, 4,710 mu of the base area in Cambodia introduced the technologies to another 14,000 mu; 1,560 mu in Myanmar to another 10,030 mu; 820 mu in Laos to another 8,000 mu; 1,565 mu in Vietnam to more than 12,000 mu.

Fig. 1 Rice Green Yield-increasing Technology Experiment
and Demonstration Project in Myanmar

2.2   Introduction and Demonstration of New Rice Varieties

A batch of new rice varieties featuring high-quality, high-yield, good resistance and strong adaptability was introduced from China to project countries for testing and screening (Fig. 2). Up to now, the project has introduced 44 rice varieties from China and selected 15 good varieties suitable for local areas. Among them, 9 of 25 introduced varieties to Cambodia were selected; 1 of 5 introduced varieties to Myanmar was selected; 2 of 11 introduced varieties to Laos were selected; all 3 varieties introduced to Vietnam were selected. At the same time, comparison tests were carried out between the introduced varieties and the local varieties.

Fig. 2   Variety Comparison Experiment of Rice Green Yield-increasing
Technology Project in China (Guangxi) -Laos Experimental
Station for Superior Crop Varieties

2.3   Experiments on Plant-breeding Models in the Paddy Field

Centering on the development of rice-shrimp, rice-fish, rice-duck and other plant-breeding models in the paddy field, the corresponding plant-breeding technologies of green rice planting were tested, demonstrated and promoted in Cambodia (Fig. 3). A total of 6 experimental varieties were introduced for plant-breeding model experiments and demonstrations of rice-shrimp, rice-fish, and rice-duck. According to the measured results, the rice-duck model increases the economic return by CNY￥ 220 per mu，with minimal input costs and risks，and low returns；the rice-fish model requires a renovation to paddy field，which has the highest input costs and risks，and high returns，reaching an increased economic return of CNY ￥413 per mu. The project plans to transform 212 mu of prawn fields in Cambodia，the implementation of rice-giant river prawn project，is expected to increase production by CNY￥ 3,000 per mu.

Fig. 3　Rice-giant River Prawn Project in Cambodia

2. 4　Personnel Training and Exhibition Promotion

Relying on the platform of China（Guangxi）-ASEAN Experimental Station for Superior Crop Varieties，the Guangxi Overseas Agricultural Cooperation Demonstration Zone，and the promoting mechanism of the agricultural cooperation institutions of the project countries，trainings on high-yield，high-quality and efficient rice cultivation techniques，disease and pest prevention and management technologies，and the use and maintenance of agricultural machinery were carried out. Up to now，more than 50 technical training sessions have been carried out，and 1,496 local farmers and technical personnel participated. China （Guangxi）-Laos Experimental Station for Superior Crop Varieties held an on-site guidance

and result demonstration and promotion event in Laos with 12 households of growers participated.

2. 5　Organizing and Optimizing Rice Green Yield-increasing Technologies for Local Regions

Green rice yield-increasing technologies were optimized according to the local situation. For example, the new technology of mechanical direct seeding of rice was optimized in Cambodia; In Laos, techniques such as centralized seedling raising, machine transplanting, water and air balance, "three-control" cultivation, precise fertilization, rice-straw returning, comprehensive management of major disease and pest have been assembled and promoted along with the establishment of a SOP of rice production and a set of technical regulations for green rice yield-increasing that were suitable for the local areas. In Myanmar, methods such as concentrated seedling cultivation to select strong seedlings, direct seeding, and seedling throwing were optimized, the application of organic fertilizer and farm manure promoted, and the use of vibration frequency insecticidal lamps and yellow boards used in the field. A pilot demonstration of direct seeding of rice was carried out in Vietnam (Fig. 4).

Fig. 4　Rice Green Yield-increasing Technology Experiment
and Demonstration Project in Vietnam

3　Achievements

3. 1　Continuous Improvement in the Application of Green Rice Yield-increasing Technology in the Lancang-Mekong Sub-region

The construction and promotion of the experiment and demonstration bases for green rice yield-increasing technology in the Lancang-Mekong sub-region has improved the application level of green rice yield-increasing technology in Cambodia, Myanmar, Laos, and Vietnam. On the whole, the project has established a total of 8, 655 mu of experiment and demonstration bases, driven another area of more than 44,030 mu of land to apply rice yield-increasing technology. On average, more than 5 mu of the local rice fields was driven to apply the technologies by each mu of the experiment and demonstration base. From the perspective of regions, each mu of experiment and demonstration base in Cambodia, Myanmar, Laos, and Vietnam promoted the application of the technology in about 3. 0 mu, 6. 4 mu, 9. 8 mu, and 7. 7 mu respectively.

3. 2　Significant Increasing of Production and Efficiency in the Lancang-Mekong Sub-region

Rice yield and efficiency in the Lancang-Mekong sub-region has been increased significantly upon the introduction and demonstration of new varieties, the promotion and application of water and fertilizer management, disease and pest prevention and management, etc. On the one hand, the introduction, testing and selection of new rice varieties featuring high-quality, high-yield, good resistance and strong adaptability provided seed quality guarantee for the improvement of rice quality and production in the Lancang-Mekong sub-region. 15 out of 44 rice varieties introduced from China were suitable for the project area. On the other hand, the promotion and application of rice green yield-increasing technology has greatly reduced the used amount of chemical fertilizers and

pesticides, improved the level of green rice production. In addition, it also reduced the losses caused by diseases and pests and the cost of prevention and management, resulting in increased yield and quality of rice, which has strengthened the market competitiveness of rice in the region. For example, the new technology of rice mechanical direct seeding adopted in Cambodia has effectively reduced pests and diseases, while increasing the rice yield by 25.9% per mu, and increasing revenue and saved costs by CNY ￥159.5. Laos, Myanmar, and Vietnam have optimized the combination of green rice yield-increasing technologies that are suitable for the local areas. Rice yields per mu increased by 47.4%, 10.2%, and 10.3% respectively, and income increased by CNY￥120, CNY￥210, and CNY￥112 respectively.

3.3　Improvement of Skills of Farmers and Technicians in the Lancang-Mekong Sub-region

The skills of farmers and technicians in the region have been improved through training on techniques such as high-yield, high-quality, high-efficiency rice cultivation techniques, disease and pest control techniques, and the use and maintenance of agricultural machinery. For farmers, technical training and promotion and demonstration have changed their traditional concepts of pest control. By simply comparing the outputs, the farmers have truly realized the role of this technology. For technicians, the application level of their related technologies of green rice production have been greatly improved after more than 50 sessions of technical training.

4　Impacts

4.1　Overseas Trials and Demonstrations Supported Industrial Cooperation

As one of the important means of agricultural cooperation with foreign countries, Lancang-Mekong Sub-regional Rice Green Yield-increasing

Technology Experiment and Demonstration Project has played an important role in deepening international exchanges and cooperation. Mature technologies such as seedling raising, cultivation, water and fertilizer management, green control of plan tpests, etc. , from China have been introduced to other countries in accordance with local conditions. Meanwhile, experiments, demonstrations and promotions of green plant-breeding models in the paddy field models have been carried out. Yield and income have been increased under the premise of protecting the local eco-environment. This provided effective technical support for promoting local rice quality and production efficiency, and also provided a scientific basis for rice scientific research and breeding.

4. 2   The Contact with Agriculture-related Departments Abroad Enhanced Foreign Affairs Service Capabilities

Through pragmatically providing many public welfare services for local rice production, this project played an active role in improving local agricultural production technology, promoting agricultural production and income, as well as serving as a component of the overall diplomacy. This was highly appreciated by the agricultural sectors of the project countries. At the same time, the demonstration bases gave full play to its local advantages of rooting in the local area and having local friends, which promoted domestic agricultural production management technicians to further understand the situation of local agriculture, rural areas, and farmers through the bases, and provided a basis for decision-making to better promote agricultural exchanges and cooperation.

5   Difficulties and Challenges

5. 1   Blocked Introduction of Seedlings Due to Policy Constraints

The project coincided with the general election in Cambodia. Ministry of Agriculture, Forestry and Fisheries of Cambodia suspended the approval

of the introduction of prawn larvae. Thus, the normal process of introduction of shrimp larvae and the experiment and demonstration of rice-prawn model were blocked, which affected the implementation of the project. At the same time, China and Cambodia did not reach an agreement on the import and export inspection and quarantine of aquatic products. This has directly stopped the project from importing giant river prawn larvae from Guangxi Institute of Fishery Sciences on time as planned. Alternatively, the seedlings were induced from Cambodia Aquatic Science Institute. As a result, the goal of selling rice-shrimp on the market was failed.

5.2　Inappropriate Varieties and Weak Supporting Facilities

After being introduced from China into Cambodia, the crayfish appeared enteritis and symptoms such as molting failure and white spot syndrome virus (WSSV) due to the difference in light, temperature, climate, and hydrological conditions, and the lack of lime in Cambodia to disinfect the pond bottom. According to expert's opinions, the second rice-shrimp experiment could not be carried out until the shrimp ditch is reconstructed. The difficulty of project implementation was usually increased due to insufficient infrastructure construction, lack of agricultural supplies, lagging early warning of natural disasters, etc., in project countries.

5.3　Weak Willingness of Local Farmers to Accept New Technologies Due to Backward Concepts

The local farmers generally hold the traditional concept of self-sufficiency in rice cultivation, and rarely use rice as a commodity. With the common belief of "live at the mercy of elements", local farmers need a process to accept new varieties and new technologies. Moreover, the current application and promotion of new technologies mainly reply on experiments and demonstrations. The current construction of demonstration bases is still limited in scope and cannot fully drive local farmers. It still takes time to promote the technology.

6 Experiences

6. 1 The Government's Attitude and Planning

The government's attitude has been an important guarantee for the smooth promotion of green rice yield-increasing cultivation technologies. The governments of Lancang-Mekong countries attached great importance to the experiment demonstration projects of green rice yield-increasing technologies. All participating parties cooperated with the local agricultural departments to establish a special project leader team to study and formulate project plans. The team carried out regular reports, follow-up implementation, on-site inspections, etc. , to track the project status and existing problems to address them.

6. 2 Responsibilities and Assessment Measures

In order to strengthen the inspection and supervision of the project and ensure the smooth completion of the project work, each related division was required to implement the work objectives and tasks one by one in accordance with the contract, and formulate specific plans for the whole year with quantified assessment indicators. Relevant government departments have raised their awareness of green rice yield-increasing cultivation technologies to promote the coverage of the technologies. The farmers were assured to have certain professional knowledge to deal with various problems during rice planting by implementing follow-up guidance, which eventually ensured the increase of yield and efficiency of rice green cultivation.

6. 3 Construction of Bases and Promotion of Technologies

The promotion and application of new technologies requires a certain process, and the experiment and demonstration of the technology is one of the important means to promote the application of it. Through the

construction of experiment and demonstration bases for green rice yield-increasing technology, this project drove surrounding growers to use new technologies. The base has brought a good radiation effect. On average, the experimental demonstration base per mu has driven the application of new technologies in rice fields of more than 5 mu, laying an important foundation for the promotion and application of the technology.

6. 4　Adjustment and Promotion of Appropriate Technologies for Local Conditions

Due to different conditions in terms of geographical location, natural endowments, and climate in different regions, there have been different characteristics of rice production. Certain differences in the level of economic development and technology application between different regions have also existed. The project carried out technical experiments and demonstrations adapted to the local characteristics, laying a solid foundation for the promotion and application of the technology, and satisfying the local green rice production technology needs at the same time.

Case 6　Demonstration of Intergration of Rubber Tree Cultivation and Processing Technology in Lancang-Mekong Countries

Natural rubber is listed as the four major industrial raw materials alongside steel, petroleum and coal. It is the only renewable resource among them and one of the most important strategic materials. However, the cultivation of rubber tree is greatly restricted by geographical environment. Most areas of the Lancang-Mekong River Basin are located in tropical, humid, and windless areas, and are also traditional cultivation areas for rubber tree with appropriate natural geographical conditions. Demonstration of Integration of Rubber Tree Cultivation and Processing Technology in Lancang-Mekong Countries Project provided rubber tree cultivation and processing technology, and carried out construction of demonstration sites in response to the increasing demand in technologies such as cultivation, latex harvest and latex processing through detailed investigation of the problems existing in the development of the natural rubber industry in Lancang-Mekong countries. This project has improved the quality of local rubber products and promoted the development of rubber industry in Lancang-Mekong countries.

1　Objectives

The natural rubber industry in some Lancang-Mekong countries has long been troubled by various backward cultivation techniques such as high incidence of diseases and pests, high incidence of tapping panel dryness (TPD), mainly focusing on natural rubber processing in traditional ribbed smoked sheet (RSS) rubber processing and production, and lack of technically specified rubber (TSR) processing technology and platform. On the other hand, China has innovative technological advantages such as

150

drought-resistant cultivation, high-yielding cultivation, TPD prevention and management, advanced rubber tapping technology and TSR (gel grade) processing technology. In order to tackle the above issues, the Rubber Research Institute of the Chinese Academy of Tropical Agricultural Sciences (CATASRRI) has cooperated with Cambodia Rubber Research Institute (CRRI), Rubber Research Institute of Vietnam (RRIV), Rubber Authority of Thailand (RAOT), Yunnan Rubber Investment CO., LTD. (Laos), Ministry of Agriculture, Livestock and Irrigation (MOALI) of Myanmar and Myanmar Rubber Planters and Producers Association (MRPPA) to select locations in core rubber producing areas of various countries to build a 30-50 mu (2-3 ha) high-yielding and high-efficiency rubber tree comprehensive cultivation technology demonstration sites, respectively. These demonstrations sites focus on demonstrating and promoting our maturely developed products and equipment such as rubber tapping technology, mini budding seedling, Sipikang (TPD Control Agents), electric rubber tapping knife, and dry rubber content (DRC) testing device. The demonstration sties provide an important platform for promoting the advancement of rubber tree cultivation and processing technology in Lancang-Mekong countries, and further deepening the cooperation of the member countries on the whole industry chain of rubber tree propagation, cultivation, tapping and processing.

2 Activities

The project has introduced, demonstrated and promoted our mature cultural practices and processing technology in accordance with the development needs of the natural rubber industry in Cambodia, Laos, Myanmar, Thailand and Vietnam. The institute also established a natural rubber tapping technology demonstration site. Further, the project introduced advanced technology and equipment, selected locations for demonstration sites and conducted technical training on selection and operation of equipment or instruments.

From June 27 to July 6, 2018, researchers visited Laos to implement the Lancang-Mekong international cooperation project to carry out research on plant diversity of the rubber plantations in Lancang-Mekong region, and provided guidance for the Laos rubber production in terms of management, rubber tapping system and yield, and the spatial distribution of rubber plantations and other typical tropical crops.

In November 2019, the Lancang-Mekong Cooperation Achievement Exhibition was held at the Laos-ITECC Exhibition Center. The exhibition helped the participating countries to better understand the development of the countries in Lancang-Mekong region. In addition, the exhibition provided more opportunities for exchanges and cooperation in the fields of rubber raw material purchasing, rubber product sales, technologies in rubber and agricultural products sectors, rubber and agricultural product inspection and quarantine, and training on rubber cultivation and rubber technology.

In the first half of 2020, China and CRRI, Myanmar Perennial Crops Division and MRPPA reached an agreement to jointly build 50 mu (3 ha) of natural rubber tapping technology demonstration sites, respectively, in the core rubber producing areas of Tboung Khmum Province, Cambodia and Yangon, Myanmar (Fig. 1). According to the differences of the two demonstration sites in demonstration of rubber cultivation, China has delivered 104 products to CRRI such as special fertilizer for rubber trees, electric rubber tapping knives, microbial fertilizers, tapping panel stimulant and Sipikang that were needed for the establishment of the demonstration sites; China also has sent to the MRPP Association 72 products including fertilizers, tapping panel stimulant, electric rubber tapping knives and dry rubber content (DRC) testing device. In response to the needs of CRRI for the production of organic fertilizers for rubber trees and the isolation and identification of leaf diseases, 5 sets of rubber tree pathology and physiology testing and analysis instruments were purchased for technical training. China also provided technical guidance for the transformation of the ribbed smoked sheet rubber processing production line and delivered five-in-one roll mill, coagulation tank and aluminum alloy plate to support the transformation and upgrade of the ribbed smoked sheet rubber processing production line of CRRI. Ten technical demonstration manuals (Tab. 1) such as *Technical Demonstration Manual for the Sipikang Series Products-TPD Control Agents by Rubber Research Institute* were pre-printed. In response to the COVID-19 pandemic, online trainings were carried out. In terms of satisfaction indicators, more than 200 scientific and technical personnel and farmers from member countries participating in the training were 100% satisfied concerning the online training. The production level of the demonstration sites was significantly improved. The production and environmental level of the sites was much higher than the local average.

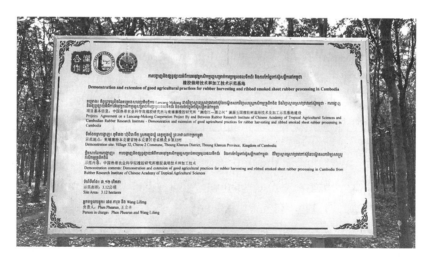

Fig. 1　Signboard for the Demonstration Site in

Chinese, English and Khmer in Cambodia

Tab. 1   Technical Demonstration Manuals for Lancang-Mekong

Cooperation Project from CATASRRI

Code	Manuals
1	Technical Demonstration Manual for the Sipikang Series Products-TPD Control Agents by Rubber Research Institute
2	Technical Demonstration Manual for the 4CJX-303B Rechargeable Lithium-ion Rotary Cutting Machine by Rubber Research Institute
3	Technical Demonstration Manual for Application of High-Efficiency Tapping Panel Stimulant to Rubber Trees by Rubber Research Institute
4	Technical Demonstration Manual for the Cordless Brushless Tapping Knife 4GXJ-2 by Rubber Research Institute
5	Technical Demonstration Manual for Detection of Dry Rubber Content（DRC）by Rubber Research Institute
6	Technical Demonstration Manual for Mini-Budding of Rubber Trees by Rubber Research Institute
7	Technical Demonstration Manual for Simplified Cultivation Techniques for Rubber Tree by Rubber Research Institute
8	Technical Demonstration Manual for Application of Slow-released Fertilizer to Rubber Trees by Rubber Research Institute
9	Technical Demonstration Manual for Rubber Tree Leaf Disease Identification
10	Technical Demonstration Manual for Production of Microbial Organic Fertilizer

In 2021，overcoming the impact of COVID-19 pandemic，the project has reached a cooperation agreement with CRRI and Yunnan Rubber Investment CO.，LTD.（Laos）through various methods such as signing agreements online，conducting online technical guidance and training demonstrations，and making operation videos and manuals to facilitate the establishment of high-yielding and high-efficiency comprehensive cultivation technology demonstration sites and the upgrading of processing and production lines.

3 Achievements

3. 1 Remarkable Results of the Establishment of the Rubber Cultivation Demonstration Sites

In 2020，CATASRRI has cooperated with CRRI，Myanmar Perennial Crops Division and MRPPA and has established a total of 100 mu (6. 6 ha) of rubber plantations for rubber tree tapping demonstration sites in Cambodia and Myanmar，which has significantly improved the production level of the demonstration sites，respectively. The production and environmental level of the demonstration sites were significantly higher than the local average，which has provided necessary conditions for the demonstration and promotion of rubber cultivation technology.

3. 2 Improved Processing Technology and Production Line

The project provided guidance on the site selection，infrastructure transformation，equipment selection，water and electricity installation，operation and commissioning of the technically specified rubber (gel grade) processing demonstration production line for the ribbed smoked sheet rubber processing plant of CRRI. The stainless-steel coagulation tanks and aluminum alloy plates provided by CATASRRI have significantly improved production efficiency. In addition，CATASRRI has provided technical support for the improvement of preliminary processing technology and the increase of production line capacity (Fig. 2).

3. 3 Remarkable Effects of Technical Training and Guidance

Training of rubber tree cultivation and primary processing technology was provided through online methods，videos，technical manuals，etc. , which has significantly improved the level of rubber production and primary processing in the five countries of Lancang-Mekong region，and demonstrated and promoted advanced technologies and equipment such as rubber tree tapping technology，mini budding，Sipikang，electric rubber

Old Coagulation Tanks in Ribbed Smoked Sheet
Rubber Processing Plant in Cambodia

New Stainless–steel Coagulation Tanks
Provided by CATASRRI

Fig. 2   Comparison of Old and New Coagulation Tanks in Cambodia's
Ribbed Smoked Sheet Rubber Processing Plant

tapping knives and dry rubber content (DRC) testing device. For example, Sipikang water agent has increased the latex yields by 3. 32 times compared with that of the local average, and the soil granular agent has increased the production by 2. 76 times, and the local rubber production technology level was improved.

3. 4   Improved the Development of the Rubber Industry in Lancang-Mekong Countries

On the one hand, local rubber output and processed product quality has been improved, which has promoted the sale and trade of rubber products, and increased economic benefits and income of rubber growers, especially the smallholders. On the other hand, the Lancang-Mekong Cooperation Achievement Exhibition provided participating countries opportunities to better understand the rubber industry in the Lancang-

Mekong countries, and provided channels for trade, cooperation and technical exchanges of rubber products in Lancang-Mekong countries.

4   Impacts

In-depth academic exchanges and cooperation have been carried out within the framework of the International Rubber Research and Development Board (IRRDB) and the Association of Natural Rubber Producing Countries (ANRPC). It also carried out cooperation such as multilateral clone exchange, technical training and academic exchanges with relevant countries in Southeast Asia. *The Agreement by and Between Cambodian Rubber Research Institute, The Kingdom of Cambodia and Rubber Research Institute, CATAS, The People's Republic of China on Rubber Research Cooperation was signed*, which has laid a good foundation for cooperation.

The cooperation activities proposed by the project are forward-looking and innovative, and meet the needs of both parties and make use of the advantages of both parties. The selected cooperation methods and implementation plans are feasible, and the arrangement of tasks and goal in the project is reasonable. This project can improve the research capacity and comprehensive innovation capabilities, and promote the development of related industries of both parties. The project has played a significant role in improving rubber tree cultivation and processing technology in Lancang-Mekong countries, connecting the Belt and Road Initiative, and promoting all-round cooperation and exchanges within the framework of the Lancang-Mekong international organization platform and subsequent in-depth technical exchanges and cooperation.

5   Difficulties and Challenges

The implementation of the project in 2020 encountered difficulties due to the ravage of the COVID-19 pandemic. Visits to Lancang-Mekong countries for technical guidance and inviting experts from these countries for training failed to be implemented as scheduled. Transportation cost has risen, resulting in the delay of the delivery of the materials to the designated countries.

In order to ensure the smooth implementation of the project, the project has actively used information technology to expand oversea partnerships, and achieved certain accomplishment. However, the progress of oversea activities in technical exchanges and experiment demonstration projects was limited. And it was not possible to invite foreign technical personnel to China for training. Considering the complexity of equipment operation and the actual effects of training, training only by online means has increased the difficulty of achieving the expected effects of the project.

6 Experiences

6.1 Carefully Organizing and Planning of the Project Implementation

The project implementing institute actively organized project planning and implementation, and coordinated and signed agreements and research plans with rubber research institutes or rubber organizations of Lancang-Mekong countries. The selection of the demonstration sites was based on the principle of selecting national rubber research institutions under relevant ministries for cooperation. They were located in the main natural rubber producing areas with the major clones of the countries. The rubber plantations selected for demonstration were planted with the major clones of the countries, and had good appearance, and the demonstrate sites are easy for access, convenient for transportation. The project implementing institutions should provide professional management of scientific research personnel and rubber workers.

6.2 Provide Targeted Technical Support Based on Preliminary Survey

The principle of the selecting demonstration technologies was based on the preliminary survey and the background of the selected sites according to different needs of the partners, and the project has designed different technologies for demonstration and prepared plans accordingly. After the demonstration sites were established, the project launched continuous track and guidance for the implementation of the project activities. For example, surveys on the distribution of natural rubber resources, tapping systems, and tapping technology were first carried out in cooperation with experts from CRRI, and Myanmar Perennial Crops Division and MRPPA. And then the partners were asked to raise technical requirements. This allowed the promotion of the development of the local rubber industry and the demonstration of technology promotion more pertinent and precise.

6.3 Promote Rubber Production Technology by Means of Technical Guidance and Equipment Guarantee

The project provided technical guidance for the upgrading of the production line for processing of ribbed smoked sheet rubber in CRRI, and provided consumables such as spare parts for five-in-one roll mill, stainless steel coagulation tanks, and aluminum alloy plates. This has supported the upgrading of production line for the ribbed smoked sheet rubber processing in CRRI from the perspectives of technology and sources. At the same time, considering the lack of local technical supporting facilities, the supporting instruments and equipment provided by CATASRRI effectively solved this problem, ensuring the technical demonstration effect, and promoting the efficiency of subsequent upgrading of processing technology.

Case 7　Lancang-Mekong Aquatic Animal Protection and Fishery Cooperation Project

The Lancang-Mekong River is the most important transnational water system in Asia, connecting six Lancang-Mekong countries. The biodiversity especially fish species ranks third in the world. In recent years, the ecological environment of the Lancang-Mekong River Basin has been deteriorating under the influence of drought, hydropower and other water-related projects, and illegal fishing. The aquatic animal resources are affected to various degrees, and the Mekong River Irrawaddy dolphins is at risk of extinction. The contradiction between economic development and ecological protection is gradually emerging. It is urgent to find a way to protect aquatic biodiversity, promote the sustainable use of resources as well as develop the economy. Lancang-Mekong Aquatic Animal Protection and Fishery Cooperation Project is organized and implemented by Office of Fisheries Law Enforcement for the Yangtze River Basin, MARA, China. In order to promote the effective development of conservation of aquatic animal resources in the Lancang-Mekong River Basin, the project focuses on various aspects including the construction of the water ecological conservation and fisheries cooperation mechanisms in the Lancang-Mekong River Basin, technical training in aquaculture, joint law enforcement, enhancement and release, and the conservation of aquatic animal resources.

1　Objectives

The project aimed to promote all-round and multi-field cooperation in the protection of water ecology in the Lancang-Mekong River Basin, and to improve the conservation level of aquatic animal resources in Lancang-Mekong countries. In addition, this project dedicated to effectively promote the construction of water ecological conservation exchange and cooperation mechanism in the Lancang-Mekong River Basin, and deepen the friendly cooperation between China and the Mekong River Basin countries in every aspect. Based on the previous results of the Lancang-Mekong cooperation, this project focused on pragmatic cooperation in aquatic animal protection and fishery cooperation to achieve the common goal of building a green Lancang-Mekong region. Lancang-Mekong Aquatic Animal Protection and Fishery Cooperation Project focused on development and cooperation and studied the green and high-quality development path of the Lancang-Mekong River Basin. The projects aimed to advance fishery ecological cooperation in the Lancang-Mekong River Basin to be upgraded every year and create a coordinated and linked Lancang-Mekong development pattern according to the model of "development-first, pragmatic and efficient, and project-oriented". In addition, the projects took advantage of scientific and technological resources of scientific research institutes to carry out technical training on fishery resource management and aquaculture development in Lancang-Mekong countries, which has improved the level of fishery resource management in Lancang-Mekong countries and the level of local fish farming. Furthermore, the projects have reduced the pressure on the use of natural fishery resources, and promoted the construction of a green economic belt in the Lancang-Mekong River Basin.

2　Activities

The project team has carried out relevant work in an orderly manner on the Lancang-Mekong Aquatic Animal Protection and Fishery Cooperation Project since 2018, which has promoted the establishment of a water ecological conservation and fisheries cooperation mechanism, and deepened the cooperation in fisheries and water ecology in the Lancang-Mekong River Basin.

2.1 Lancang-Mekong River Basin Biological Resources Conservation Forum Co-sponsored with International Organizations

In November 2018, MARA hosted the Lancang-Mekong River Basin Biological Resources Conservation Forum with the theme of "Developing Sustainable Fisheries and Building a Harmonious Lancang-Mekong River Basin" which aims to actively implement the Belt and Road Initiative and the deployment of the Lancang-Mekong Cooperation (Fig. 1). Over 70 officials, experts and scholars affiliated with various organizations gathered together to discuss the conservation of ecological resources and promotion of the sustainable development of fisheries in the Lancang-Mekong River Basin. All participants actively discussed over various topics and reached a number of consensuses on the protection of aquatic animal resources in the region and the establishment of a long-term Lancang-Mekong cooperation mechanism. The success of the forum has preliminarily established a work pattern of "governments leading, firms cooperating, public participating and international society supporting".

Fig. 1　Group Photo of Participants in the Sub-forum on Biological Resources Conservation in the Lancang-Mekong River Basin

2. 2　Memorandum of Cooperation with Cambodia to Reach a Consensus

In 2017, the Office of Fisheries Law Enforcement for the Yangtze River Basin and the Fisheries Bureau of the Ministry of Agriculture, Forestry and Fisheries of Cambodia signed the *Memorandum of Cooperation on the Conservation of Lancang-Mekong Aquatic Animal Resources Between China and Cambodia*. A consensus on cooperation has been reached on in-situ and ex-situ protection of Irrawaddy dolphins, fishery stock enhancement and release, resource and environmental monitoring, an information exchange mechanism and a joint fishery law enforcement system, thus to jointly strengthen the protection of aquatic biological resources and water ecology in the Lancang-Mekong River Basin.

2. 3　Significant Progress in the Lancang-Mekong Joint Enhancement and Release

Enhancement and release were one of the 45 early harvest projects of the Lancang-Mekong cooperation mechanism. In 2017, China coordinated with the fishery administrative authorities of Laos, Cambodia, Thailand and other countries to jointly carry out enhancement and release projects. A total of 2.193 million fish fries were released with a completion rate of 365.5%, which exceeded the project targets. By participating in the 16th National Fish Release Day in Cambodia in July 2018, the project exchanged views with the Ministry of Agriculture, Forestry and Fisheries of Cambodia on aquatic animal protection cooperation under the framework of the Lancang-Mekong cooperation mechanism (Fig. 2). In 2018, the project carried out multiple enhancement and release activities in Thailand in May, in Cambodia in July, and Xishuangbanna, Yunnan Province of China in November. On July 10, 2019, the project launched the 2019 China-Laos joint law enforcement and enhancement and release activity in Xishuangbanna, Yunnan Province with Ministry of Natural Resources and Environment of Laos, the Department of Natural Resources and

Environment of Luang Namtha Province, the Department of Agriculture and Rural Affairs of Yunnan Province, the Agricultural and Rural Bureau of Xishuangbanna Prefecture. On July 13-14, 2019, this project participated in the "March 8" (a natural reserve supported by women in Nanta River) enhancement and release activity in Luang Namtha Province, Laos and donated 230,000 fish fries to Luang Namtha Province, including 200,000 carps, 20,000 Asian redtail catfish, and 10,000 Barbodes daruphani luosuoensis. This is the fifth time that China participated in the Fish Release Day of the Aquatic Wildlife Conservation Day in Luang Namtha Province. In the past five years, a total of 614,000 fish for enhancement and release have been donated, including 560,000 carp, 44,000 Asian redtail catfish, and 10,000 Barbodes daruphani luosuoensis, which has greatly protected and supplemented the aquatic animal resources in the basin (Fig. 3).

Fig. 2　Signing Ceremony of *Memorandum of Cooperation on the Conservation of Lancang-Mekong Aquatic Animal Resources Between China and Cambodia*

2.4　Scientific Investigation of the Mekong River Irrawaddy Dolphins

In 2019, two scientific investigations of the Mekong River Irrawaddy dolphins were carried out in the Mekong River in Cambodia (Fig. 4). It

Fig. 3　The Artificial Release in 2019

was found that the Mekong River Irrawaddy dolphins were mainly distributed in 4‐6 deep water areas in the Mekong River in Cambodia. The cumulative population of the Mekong River Irrawaddy dolphins in this section was estimated to be 76‐80 individuals. The scientific investigation has strengthened the cooperation and exchanges between China and Cambodia in the protection of endangered species and resource conservation in the Lancang-Mekong River Basin，and effectively promoted the smooth implementation of the Lancang-Mekong Aquatic Animal Protection and Fishery Cooperation Project.

Fig. 4　Group Photo of the Survey Team on the Mekong River
　　　　Irrawaddy Dolphins Population

2. 5 Deepened Cooperation in Fishery Administration and Law Enforcement Between China and Laos

In November 2015, China and Laos launched the first joint Lancang-Mekong fishery administration and law enforcement action, which has created a new pattern of joint law enforcement between the two countries' fishery administration. In addition, the cooperation opened a new chapter in the joint management and conservation of the Lancang-Mekong aquatic animal resources and ecological environment, and established a long-term cooperation mechanism. In December 2017, China and Laos jointly launched the "2017 China-Laos Lancang-Mekong Fishery Administration and Law Enforcement Action and Enhancement and release Activity". In order to protect the aquatic animal resources and water ecological environment in the Lancang-Mekong region, the two sides have established a mechanism of regular visits and focused on multiple aspects including continuously strengthening communication, building consensus, and deepening cooperation. In 2018, nearly a hundred pieces or sets of electric fish tools or nets confiscated in border waters were destroyed, and 70,000 local fish fries were released. In July 2019, China and Laos carried out joint fishery law enforcement actions and aquatic animal enhancement and release activities in the Lancang-Mekong Basion for the fifth consecutive year. At the event, the project destroyed various illegal fishing equipment including 60 sets of electric fishing machines, 36 ground cages, 110 fishing nets, 1 electric trawl net, and 1 Muro-ami. A total of 200,000 Hong Kong Catfish, 100,000 Asian redtail catfish, and 15,000 Barbodes daruphani luosuoensis were released, which has further promoted the restoration of the Lancang-Mekong aquatic resources. In addition, the activities have strengthened bilateral cooperation between China and Laos, and enhanced the friendship between the two peoples. After the event, the law enforcement officers of the two countries took the No. 060 ship to carry out joint law enforcement cruise to ensure the effect of enhancement and release (Fig. 5).

Fig. 5　Group Photo of the Joint Law Enforcement Team

2.6　Preparation for the Establishment of the Water Ecological Conservation and Fisheries Cooperation Mechanism in the Lancang-Mekong River Basin

Due to the COVID-19 pandemic, the conference that was originally scheduled on February 2020 could not be held on time. It was aimed for establishing the water ecological conservation and fisheries cooperation mechanism in the Lancang-Mekong River Basin. The conference preparatory team has drafted a work plan as well as other related documents including the fishery and aquatic ecology cooperation charter (draft) in Lancang-Mekong River Basin, memorandum, framework agreement, *Wuxi Declaration*, etc. The team has communicated with Lancang-Mekong countries via email to further improve the cooperation mechanism. In addition, the team has discussed many times with relevant domestic units and departments on the work related to the conference schedules, and organized domestic experts and scholars to discuss and improve relevant materials.

3 Achievements

3.1 Economic Benefits

The fishery and aquatic ecologies have been effectively improved in the six countries in the Lancang-Mekong River Basin including Cambodia, China, Laos, Myanmar, Thailand, and Vietnam through the implementation of this project, which has carried out fishery and aquatic ecological cooperation with a gradually improved the water ecological conservation and fisheries cooperation mechanism. Meanwhile, it helped Mekong countries to improve their water ecological conservation capabilities, and provided data support for the restoration and conservation of fishery resources in the basin. Data was also set as references for the fishery development of Lancang-Mekong countries, so that they can avoid unnecessary investment and losses.

3.2 Ecological Benefits

Through this project, the water ecological conservation capacity of the six countries has been effectively improved, and the water ecological resources of the Lancang-Mekong River Basin have been jointly protected. Joint law enforcement actions have effectively protected fishery and aquatic ecological resources by banning illegal nets and cracking down on illegal fishing activities. The level of protection on aquatic animals has been improved from both theoretical and practical aspects. The project has promoted the cooperation between China and foreign countries in the protection of aquatic animals and cooperation in fishery, which has brought significant ecological benefits.

3.3 Social Benefits

This project is an important deployment to ensure the implementation of the Lancang-Mekong Cooperation Mechanism. The project comprehensively considered the needs for domestic development as well as the needs of the Mekong countries, and promoted cooperation in aquatic animal protection and fishery cooperation between China and Mekong countries by taking full advantage of the advanced capital, technology, and human resources of China. Meanwhile, the project comes with other significant social benefits such as enhancing the public satisfaction on the water environment and raising the awareness of protection, publicizing fishery ecology and biodiversity conservation.

4　Impacts

This project mainly brought about the following two impacts:

4.1　Presenting China's Image as a Responsible Major Country

This project is a concrete result of joint efforts with the Mekong countries, following Xi Jinping Thought on Diplomacy, putting the principle of amity, sincerity, mutual benefit and inclusiveness into practice, and upholding the right approach to justice and interests by putting justice at the first place. As the important work content of the concrete implementation of *Lancang-Mekong Cooperation Five-Year Action Plan (2018-2022)*, the project is an important measure to further strengthen the Lancang-Mekong water ecological conservation cooperation and share the achievements of China's water ecological protection and resource conservation in large river basins. This project mainly focused on benefiting the people of the river basin and contributing to the prosperity of the region. The implementation of the project ensures the establishment of a water ecological conservation exchange and cooperation platform in the Lancang-Mekong River Basin, which can promote the protection of the water ecology and fishery resources in the Lancang-Mekong River Basin, and enhance the friendship between the six countries.

4.2　Promoting the Sustainable Development of Fisheries in the Lancang-Mekong River Basin

This project is conducive to improving the national aquatic ecological protection and management capabilities of the Lancang-Mekong River

Basin, and raises the awareness of relevant national officials and ordinary people on the protection of aquatic animals. In order to ensure the coordinated development of protection and utilization, the project focused on the establishment of the Mekong River Irrawaddy dolphin protection and the development of eco-tourism. In return, the people's livelihood and well-being of the Lancang-Mekong countries have been effectively improved. In addition, the breadth and effectiveness of the water ecological protection of the Lancang-Mekong countries have been enhanced, and the sustainable development of fishery in the Lancang-Mekong River Basin has been promoted.

5 Difficulties and Challenges

5.1 Project Implementation Affected by the COVID-19 Pandemic

Due to the continued impact of the COVID-19 pandemic, follow-up projects need to change the way of implementation. For example, joint law enforcement was changed to simultaneous law enforcement; training was changed from offline to online; Mekong River Irrawaddy dolphin inspection and fishery resource survey will be entrusted to local fishery personnel. It is expected to have a negative impact on the effect of the project, and it cannot be changed in the short term.

5.2 Progress of Project Implementation Affected by Subjective and Objective Factors

During the project, there were still problems with all parties in terms of implementation and communication efficiency. Also, the climate in Lancang-Mekong countries is complicated, and the crossover of the rainy and dry seasons has increased the difficulty of the implementation.

5.3 Cooperation Upgrading Affected by Limited Technical Research Capability

The collection and sorting of important fish germplasm resources in the Lancang-Mekong River Basin is affected by uncertainties in the processing, identification and analysis methods of specimens and genetic samples. At the same time, professional research is mainly conducted in China. By contrast, the research on fishery resources and the protection of endangered aquatic animal resources in the Lancang-Mekong River Basin are relatively at a disadvantage. Cooperation in the field of fisheries is fragmented, and communication channels are not yet fully developed. The establishment of a water ecological conservation and fisheries cooperation mechanism in the Lancang-Mekong River Basin is not done yet due to the lack of a cooperative evaluation system.

6 Experiences

Shared River, Shared Future. Since the implementation of Lancang-Mekong Aquatic Animal Protection and Fishery Cooperation Project in 2018, it has withstood the test of the international and regional vicissitudes and the COVID-19 pandemic. We have created a coordinated development pattern that takes into account all aspects including adhering to people's livelihood and focusing on biodiversity conservation to ensure a win-win cooperation with an ecologically oriented and technology-driven development. The six countries in the Lancang-Mekong River Basin have been working together closely to promote cooperation in water ecological conservation, which have made important contributions to enhancing the well-being of the people of member countries and promoting regional sustainable fishery development.

6. 1 Eco-oriented Project

Carrying out the conservation of aquatic animal resources in the Lancang-Mekong River Basin helped the protection of the Mekong River Irrawaddy dolphins and the conservation of aquatic animal resources, which promoted the sustainable use of aquatic animal resources, and protected the aquatic biodiversity during the development. An eco-oriented transnational green economic pattern has been created.

6. 2 Technology-driven Development

The project has comprehensively considered the water ecological protection and resource conservation needs of China and the Mekong countries. The Chinese government sent a core technical team to conduct a series of studies mainly on biodiversity conservation and other aspects. A large number of outstanding outputs were obtained to provide technical support for the practical cooperation to achieve the goal of building a green Lancang-Mekong region.

6. 3 Win-win Cooperation

The six Lancang-Mekong countries are connected geographically, physically, and culturally. In order to promote people's livelihood, we worked on vigorously enhancing the water ecological conservation and fisheries cooperation machanism in the Lancang-Mekong River Basin in a broader field and a deeper level with pragmatic actions and heart-to-heart measures. Gathering people's intelligence and strength and conducting mutually beneficial and win-win cooperation, we will jointly embark on a path of green development.

Case 8　Demonstration Zone Project for Cooperation on Tropical Agricultural Industrialization of Lancang-Mekong Area

Most of the countries and regions in the Lancang-Mekong River Basin have tropical or subtropical climates, and agriculture is the traditional pillar industry. The area, though blessed with relative abundance of its natural resources, lags behind in agricultural modernization, and S&T-driven growth accounts for a meager portion of that of the agricultural sector. One of the daunting tasks this region is facing currently is to find a way to improve the comprehensive production capacity, international competitiveness and sustainable development capacity of tropical agricultural industry by taking advantage of the resources of the tropical zone, and finally transform and upgrade the traditional agriculture to modern agriculture. Demonstration Zone Project for Cooperation on Tropical Agricultural Industrialization of Lancang-Mekong Area aims to explore the path of tropical agriculture modernization in the Lancang-Mekong region from a strategic perspective with a regional platform supportive of cooperation on industrialization of tropical agriculture, towards a new multinational industrial pattern in which tropical crop resources are expected to play complementary roles between countries.

1　Objectives

By cooperating with local Cambodian enterprises and using proven Chinese technology of water and fertilizer integrated irrigation and scientific and standardized agricultural industrialization management model, the project gave full play to the advantages of the scientific and technological resources in Chinese scientific research institutes to carry out the training of tropical agriculture talents in the region. This project has

173

promoted the development and interregional cooperation of local industries including banana, pepper, coconut, mango, etc. and driven the common development of agriculture and rural economy in the Lancang-Mekong region, which can help build a community of shared future among Lancang-Mekong countries.

The main goal of the project is to establish "one hub, multiple parks and bases". Among them, one hub refers to the 200, 000 mu core demonstration hub of Oasis Agricultural Development (Cambodia) Co., Ltd. located in Kratie Province, Cambodia. Multiple parks refer to the construction of large-scale and modern industrial demonstration parks by selecting adaptable tropical agricultural varieties and building a full-industry chain operation and management team with relatively complete production factors. Multiple bases refer to establishment of standardized agricultural production bases. The project will guide foreign, domestic and local enterprises in accordance with local conditions to construct those bases.

2　Activities

A series of tropical agricultural technology exchange and cooperation activities with a focus on the tropical specific agricultural industry in the Lancang-Mekong region were carried out.

2.1　Tropical Agricultural Technology Exchanges and Human Resources Training

First, there has been a total of nearly 300 delegates consisting of competent officials, entrepreneurs, and technical experts sent on an official mission to the demonstration hub in Kratie Province, Cambodia to advise on overseas investment issues. Second, the project held two training courses for Lancang-Mekong agricultural talents. One of the courses was held in Hainan Province with participants invited from 5 countries in the Lancang-Mekong region. The other course organized

Chinese experts to visit Cambodia to offer guidance. Agricultural technical and managing personnel from Lancang-Mekong countries was organized to participate in this training. Third, this project held 4 China-Cambodia tropical agricultural technology training courses with a total of about 300 trainees. Fourth, the project held 3 pepper high-yield technology training activities with a total of about 150 trainees.

2. 2　Demonstration Core Bases in Support of Cooperation on Scaled-up Agricultural Production

Building on an interplay of administrative guidelines and market-based incentives where businesses come into play as the key driver, public institutions and cooperatives as the service provider and farmers as the beneficiary, the establishment of the demonstration zone is well on track to encompass a proposed network of "one hub, multiple parks and bases". As of May 2020, the following construction has been completed: ① 15,000 mu of coconut industry cooperation core demonstration base including 50 mu of coconut germplasm resource nursery; ②5,000 mu of banana industry cooperation core demonstration base (Fig. 1, Fig. 2); ③1,000 mu of pepper industry cooperation core demonstration base

Fig. 1　Banana Industry Cooperation Core Demonstration Base

Fig. 2　Solar Photovoltaic Water Control Irrigation System
in Banana Industry Cooperation Core Demonstration Base

(Fig. 3）；④ 10,000 mu of rubber industry core demonstration base；
⑤ 10,000 mu of mango industry cooperation core demonstration base；
⑥10,000 mu of teak industry cooperation core demonstration base；⑦ 300
mu of cashew industry cooperation core demonstration base．Meanwhile，
the project also upgraded and transformed infrastructures including leveling

Fig. 3　Pepper Industry Cooperation Core Demonstration Base

50,000 mu of land, purchasing more than 200 sets of agricultural and forestry machineries, building more than 200 kilometers of park roads, 20,000 m² of factories and 2,000 m² of offices and living areas, accessing to Cambodia's national public grid, constructing five small and medium-sized reservoirs, with a water supply capacity of more than 20 million m³ in the dry season.

2.3 Ecological Protection in the Demonstration Zone

A new model of tropical ecological agriculture development in the Lancang-Mekong region that combines "ecological protection+agricultural development" was created. The project cooperated with an environmental protection agency to formulate an ecological environment and biodiversity protection plan for the demonstration area, and delineate the ecological protection red line. 120,000 mu of tropical virgin forest were planned to be used for ecological conservation, and 80,000 mu of land for agricultural planting and construction of reservoirs, roads, processing areas, office and living areas. In addition, ecological corridors for animal and plant conservation were delineated to formulate a spot-type development module. The forest coverage rate was maintained as more than 60% and vegetation coverage rate more than 90% in the core demonstration base (Fig. 4).

Fig. 4 Wild Animals Protected in the Demonstration Zone

3 Achievements

3. 1 Roles of Tropical Crops Production Established in Cambodia with Clear Lines of Demarcation Drawn Regarding Lands Suitable for Crop Production

Re-investigation and regional planning of Cambodia's new tropical crop industry resources were carried out. By clarifying suitable areas for planting in Cambodia, the blind convergence of the tropical crop industry structure adjustment was avoided. The government's guidance was intensified to vigorously support the agricultural pillar industries. For example, a comprehensive development pattern of "dots to lines, and lines to areas" has been formed for the industries of coconut, banana, pepper, and mango in Cambodia. Networking and electronation of market information, pests and diseases forecasting have been conducted.

3. 2 Introduction of High-quality Fruit Varieties and Improvement of Seed Varieties

Cambodia has actively changed the current situation of single germplasm structure by introducing high-quality fruit varieties and optimizing the structure of seed varieties. The nursery construction and seed resource collection have been completed for the 50 mu coconut germplasm resource nursery project. In addition, Cambodia has accelerated the transformation of old orchards of mango, coconut, etc. The project has vigorously promoted the existing plant shrinkage and dwarfing technology to promote industrial upgrading and improve product quality. Meanwhile, strengthened emphasis on post-production processing in Cambodia for value-added products and extended industrial chains has given it a competitive edge that has earned itself a bigger share of the international market.

3.3 Introduction of Standardized Production and Changes of the Industrial Business Model

Cambodia has changed the development mode from extensive operation to a modern order-based agricultural business model of "enterprise + farmer". They have improved product quality and reduced costs by implementing brand strategy and integration of production, supply and marketing, which has enhanced market competitiveness of their products. In addition, a standardized management system has been gradually formed. Through taking measures such as unified standard management, unified material supply, and unified brand management, the project has built a large-scale green agricultural product production base, which has cultivated several agricultural industries and enterprises with international competitiveness. In return, standardization and industrialization of Cambodian agricultural industry have been greatly improved. This also established the whole industry chain. A number of professional enterprises have been successively attracted to jointly build a whole industry chain cluster surrounding the banana industry in Cambodia. It has formed a complete industrial chain structure with complete supporting facilities, including technical services for water and fertilizer integrated irrigation facilities, organic fertilizer production services, logistics services, food security inspection and quarantine services, tissue culture seedling technology production services, and carton packaging services.

3.4 Improved Infrastructure and Professional Education Platform Put into Service

Beefed-up financing has gone to hardware facilities and a well functioned professional training platform in response to the needs of regional layout and specialized production. At present, the hardware investments of the 15,000 mu of coconut industry cooperation core demonstration base such as land leveling, digging ponds for irrigation, road rolling, construction of power facilities, and construction of production houses have completed. Other works such as coconut seedling nursery, digging pits to plant, and laying of water and fertilizer integrated irrigation facilities have been completed as well. The construction of talent cultivation system was steadily promoted in accordance with the targeted tasks. The training class work was also connected with the base industry construction. From March to December 2020, a total of 6 training courses on monitoring, early warning, and comprehensive prevention and management of tropical agricultural pests and disease have been held. The courses offered have been a successful example in terms of the innovative teaching and the outcomes achieved as a result of the demand analysis, which represents a concrete step towards overall establishment of a professional education system for the countries of Lancang-Mekong area.

4 Impacts

4.1 The Project Has Established the Important Position of Agricultural Science and Technology Cooperation in the Tropical Agricultural Industry Cooperation in the Lancang-Mekong Region

Through sharing agricultural technology development experience with Mekong countries and promoting high-quality varieties, agricultural machineries, and cultivation management techniques, the yield of some varieties has doubled or more. At the same time, the training courses on agricultural technology and management have effectively promoted the tropical agricultural technology cooperation in the Lancang-Mekong Area, which has also improved local agricultural productivity.

4.2 The Project Has Broadened the Areas of Agricultural Cooperation between ASEAN Countries and China

Tropical agricultural industry cooperation has developed to various

links on the industrial chain including processing, warehousing, logistics, and trade, involving a variety of agricultural products such as grain (rice), economic crops (rubber, palm, cassava, sugar cane), etc. And it is expanding rapidly. This will give full play to the geographical and industrial advantages of each side to achieve China-ASEAN Strategic Partnership Vision 2030, and to promote a more rational allocation of regional resources, manpower and funds, which has promoted the industrial upgrading of the region and countries in the fields of infrastructure, agricultural processing, etc.

4.3　The Project Has Promoted Employment of Local Farmers and People-to-people Exchanges

The accomplishment and operation of China-Cambodia banana industry project will bring more than 6 billion yuan of labor services income as well as other related consumption income to the local and provide more than 100,000 job positions, which would be a huge contribution to the improvement of local people's livelihood. This will help foster harmonious neighborhood where Chinese and Cambodians come together and thrive as one family (Fig. 5).

Fig. 5　Provided Job Opportunities for Cambodian
People to Improve Their Livelihood

5 Difficulties and Challenges

5.1 Lack of Momentum for Advancing Tropical Agricultural Processing

The added value of primary agricultural products is low. However, the added value of these agricultural products will greatly increase after the secondary deep processing. Apart from the technical reasons, neither China nor the Mekong countries have paid enough attention to the processing of agricultural products. Most tropical agricultural products are either unprocessed or roughly processed, and only a small part of it is refined. The energy and material consumption of enterprises are high, and the output efficiency is low.

5.2 Shortfall in Funding of a Full Quality Traceability System

The project urgently needs to support enterprises to build agro-product quality inspection and quarantine centers in Cambodia and establish a full traceability system. With a validated product inspection, quarantine, and process quality monitoring system, countries can ensure that agricultural products meet the quality and safety requirements of exporting and importing countries.

6 Experiences

6.1 Practical Steps to Advance Industrialization

By expanding the scope of technical cooperation and strengthen the connection between government, institutes, and enterprises, scientific research results have been successfully transformed into industry-scale investment, enabling laboratory technology to be mass-produced and increasing the industrial developing space and value. In addition, Cambodia has created some international brands by learning and making full use of the advanced tropical agricultural science and technology of other Lancang-Mekong countries to strengthen its technological innovation and

accelerate the development and improvement of tropical agricultural products and varieties. Through the application of information technology，member countries can better guide the production of marketable agro-products and increase farmers' income.

6. 2   Human Resources Training as Building Bridges of Exchange and Cooperation

Cooperation was promoted through training，which represents the obvious overall benefits of the project. Agricultural technology training gave full play to the comprehensive benefits of the project and directly promoted the effective connection between scientific research institutes and Lancang-Mekong local enterprises，which led to the establishment of an overall pattern of industrial cooperation. In addition，the project conducted targeted research on talent needs and cooperation mechanisms based on the combination of technical training，return visits and investigations，which has further promoted the sustainable development of tropical agricultural cooperation in the Lancang-Mekong region both the theoretically and practically.

6. 3   A New Pathway Where Agricultural Development Is Aligned with Ecological Conservation

As a result of the endeavors to deal with agricultural development without compromising the principle of eco-friendliness，progress has been made on agricultural industrialization in parallel to a well-preserved environment for the local communities，whose embrace of the philosophy of sustainability has been laying the groundwork for any successful cooperation to take place in the long run.

Chapter 3 | Capacity Building

Case 9　Human Resources Cooperative Development System Construction and Training Project for Lancang-Mekong Countries

1　Objectives

With the advancement and deepening of the Lancang-Mekong cooperation mechanism, high-quality cooperation in various fields put forward higher requirements for human resources support and the importance of strengthening human resource development cooperation among Lancang-Mekong countries has become increasingly prominent. In recent years, the Lancang-Mekong agricultural cooperation capacity building project has been steadily carried out, mainly including the aspects as following:

Talent Training Project on Tropical Agriculture for Lancang-Mekong Countries, mainly focusing on agricultural industry management and technology training, as well as human resource cooperation, agricultural scientific and technological poverty reduction, supporting enterprise going global, training base construction, talent needs mechanism research and so on, promotes the agricultural development and rural revitalization in the countries along the Lancang-Mekong river, builds the model projects of training in Lancang-Mekong agricultural cooperation.

Transboundary Animal Disease Laboratory Diagnosis and Testing Technology Training and Demonstration Project for Lancang-Mekong countries aimed to actively serve and integrate into the Belt and Road Initiative and provide technical support for the orderly advancement of the pilot work in the foot-and-mouth disease management zone at the border in Yunnan and the standardization of cross-border movement of livestock to establish the safe trade corridors and promote legal trade in livestock and poultry.

Training Course on Biogas Technology for Countries along the Mekong River focused on the promotion of biogas technology as a promising means for the sustainable development of the region. Activities were conducted with trainees, including lectures, on-site practice, study tour to demonstration, visits to enterprises and experience sharing. As follow-ups, two projects were established and completed successfully with trainees' cooperation, namely, a UNIDO-supported project entitled "Training Course on Commercial Biogas for Cambodia" at Royal University of Cambodia, and a G77 PGTF-supported project "Installation and Demonstration of FRP Digester in Rural Remote Area" in the Philippines. Hence, the training course was a platform for mutual communication and a window to subsequent cooperation.

Capacity Building Seminar on Pesticide Risk Management for Lancang-Mekong Countries aimed at strengthening the experience exchange in pesticide risk management among Lancang-Mekong countries, and improve regional pesticide risk management capabilities, which could ensure the implementation of the Belt and Road Initiative. By sharing the common risks and challenges faced by the Lancang-Mekong countries in the field of pesticide risk management as well as China's progress and methods in this field, to the project strengthened cooperation in pesticides and other related fields for the Lancang-Mekong countries, improved regional pesticide risk management capabilities and promoted the sustainable development of agriculture in the Lancang-Mekong region.

2 Activities

2.1 Implement Six Phases of Agricultural Industry Management and Technology Training for the Countries Along the Lancang-Mekong River

From May to September, 2018, Training Course on Monitoring,

Early Warning and Integrated Management of Pests and Diseases in Tropical Agriculture, Seminar on Standards and Testing Technology for Quality and Safety of Tropical Agricultural Products, Training Course on Production and Processing of Special Tropical Cash Crops, Training Course on the Planning and Design of Modern Agricultural Industrial Park and the Application of Agricultural Informatization, Training Course on Technologies for Scale Farming of Tropical Livestock and Forage Crops Planting (Fig. 1), Seminar on "One Village One Product" for Sustainable Development of Modern Agriculture were held with 10 days duration of each training, and there were 124 participants of administrative and technical staff from governments, colleges and universities, research institutions and agricultural enterprises from Cambodia, Laos, Myanmar, Thailand and Vietnam.

Fig. 1 Closing Ceremony for Training Course on Technologies for
Scale Farming of Tropical Livestock and Forage Crops Planting

Trainings are oriented on technological needs, invite the experts with rich international cooperation experience to give the lectures, as well as lead the participants to visit the demonstration bases and feel the Chinese traditional culture, in order to lay a solid foundation for whole construction of Talent Training Project on Tropical Agriculture for the Countries along the Lancang-Mekong River.

2. 2 Transboundary Animal Disease (TAD) Laboratory Diagnosis and Testing Technical Training

The "Inviting In" task of Lancang-Mekong Cooperation (LMC) TAD Laboratory Diagnosis and Testing Technical Training, one of Lancang-Mekong Cooperation Special Fund Projects, was carried out in Kunming, Xishuangbanna, Qujing, from June 11-24, 2018 (Fig. 2). Twelve laboratory technicians from Laos, Myanmar, Thailand and Vietnam participated the training at invitation.

Fig. 2　Group Photo of Transboundary Animal Disease Laboratory Diagnosis and Testing Technical Training

At the invitation of the Bureau of Livestock and Aquatic Products of the Ministry of Agriculture and Forestry of Laos, 3 technical experts from Yunnan Academy of Animal Husbandry and Veterinary Sciences formed a "Group of Transboundary Animal Diseases Laboratory Diagnosis and Testing Technology Demonstration and Training to Laos" to carry out the training in Vientiane Province and Sainyabuli Province in Laos (Fig. 3). 25 Lao veterinary technicians were trained, which completed part of the "Going Out" exchange and cooperation tasks of the Lancang-Mekong Cooperation Special Fund Projects.

Fig. 3   Foot-and-mouth Disease Diagnosis Technology Training
in Vientiane Province and Sainyabuli Province in Laos

At the invitation of the Planning Statistics International and Information Technology Division of the Bureau of Animal Husbandry and Veterinary Medicine of the Ministry of Agriculture, Livestock and Irrigation of Myanmar, a team of technical experts formed by the Yunnan Academy of Animal Husbandry and Veterinary Sciences went to Myanmar and Thailand to carry out the "Going Out" exchange and cooperation task of Lancang-Mekong Transboundary Animal Disease Prevention and Control Technology on Dec 4-12, 2018. In conjunction with the Yunnan-aid-Myanmar project "Myanmar Cattle Foot-and-mouth Disease Diagnosis and Detection Technology Training", the team went to Yangon and Naypyidaw, Myanmar to hold cattle foot-and-mouth disease diagnostic technology training from January 6 to 19, 2019. 23 technicians in

189

Yangon, Naypyidaw, and Mandalay were trained and a laboratory cooperation agreement was signed.

2.3 Training Course on Biogas Technology for Countries Along the Mekong River

The specific preparations of the Training Course on Biogas Technology for Countries along the Mekong River were undertaken by the Training Center of Biogas Institute of Ministry of Agriculture and Rural Affairs, P. R. C. A detailed and thorough implementation plan for security work was formulated, and the *Emergency Plan for International Training Courses* and *Duties of Personnel for Training Courses* were drawn up. Mission notices were sent to international non-governmental organizations such as the United Nations Industrial Development Organization and the Asia-Pacific Biogas Alliance to recruit candidates. Applicants with professional background and work experience in related fields were selected as the final candidates.

The training course was successfully held in Chengdu from March 21 to April 3, 2018. 21 trainees from 5 countries including Cambodia, Myanmar, Laos, Thailand and Vietnam participated in the 14 day training. A specific schedule was formulated in line with the themes and the needs of the trainees during the training. Experts with rich teaching and work experience in the Biogas Institute were invited as lecturers. The project manager also actively communicated with the lecturers, to stress the quality of lectures and updates of teaching materials.

2.4 Lancang-Mekong Pesticide Risk Management Seminar

Lancang-Mekong Pesticide Risk Management Seminar was held from July 15 to August 4, 2019, which lasted three weeks. Training and inspection activities were carried out respectively in Beijing, Guangxi, and Yunnan, China. The main activities included lectures by experts, visits to laboratories of the Institute for the Control of Agrochemicals, Ministry of Agricultural and Rural Affairs of China, inspections of pesticide companies, visits to ecological agricultural industrial parks, and cultural exchanges (Fig. 4, Fig. 5). The 28 trainees who participated in the training were from the relevant agricultural departments and scientific research institutions of Thailand, Cambodia, Vietnam, Myanmar, and Laos.

Fig. 4 Experts and Trainees Discussing and Exchanging Ideas

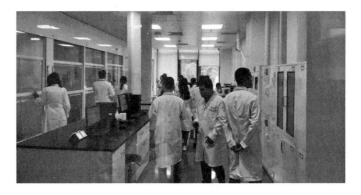

Fig. 5 Visiting the Laboratory of a Pesticide Company

During the lectures, China worked with various teaching experts and cooperative units to formulate a scientific and detailed teaching plan for the training. The content covered China's pesticide management policy and environmental risk control, China's pesticide risk management methods, China's pesticide registration and approval process, pesticide residues, biodiversity and pest control, new advances in the biological control of plant pests. The multi-dimensional and multi-level topics guaranteed the breadth and depth of the lectures, which enriched the students' knowledge of pesticides.

During the visit and inspection session, the trainees are organized to go to the enterprises for on-site investigations. The trainees also conducted visits and study exchanges in Nanning, Beihai, Guangxi, Kunming, Yunnan and surrounding cities and counties, so that the trainees gained a more intuitive and deeper understanding of pesticide risk management methods of pesticide companies, ecological agriculture, and green prevention and control in China.

3 Achievements

3.1 Expanding Agricultural Human Resources and Building Circle of Lancang-Mekong Cooperation Friends

In 2018, China implemented the Talent Training Project on Tropical Agriculture for the Countries along the Lancang-Mekong River, and carried out 6 phases of agricultural industry management and technology training. A total of 124 Lancang-Mekong agricultural management officials, agricultural technical experts and managers of agricultural enterprises have been trained, and a training base for tropical agriculture talents for the countries along the Lancang-Mekong River has been constructed. It has built 13 high-quality training courses and selected 9 training and practice bases, one Lancang-Mekong training data management system has been established with improved training management mechanism and supporting systems, and the letter of cooperation intent about technology talents for training with Ministry of Labour and Vocational Training of Cambodia has been signed.

3.2 Establishing a Sustainable Cooperation and Exchange Mechanism and Advancing Normalization of Cooperation and Exchanges

The normalization of cooperation and exchanges among Lancang-

Mekong countries has been promoted through the signing of cooperation agreements, the establishment of a mechanism for mutual visits of personnel, survey on the development of talents, follow-up training for follow-up personnel, etc. A long-term and sustainable cooperation and exchange mechanism for grassroots agricultural technology promotion personnel have been established. For example, the Yunnan Academy of Animal Husbandry and Veterinary Sciences signed a technical cooperation agreement with the National Foot-mouth Disease Laboratory in Naypyidaw, Myanmar to establish a long-term cooperative relationship which has promoted bilateral cooperation in the prevention and management of China-Myanmar cross-border animal diseases, and improved Yunnan's influence in the field of international animal health. Experts were invited by Cambodian trainees to hold the first phase (May 25th to June 1st, 2018) and the second phase (June 25th to July 5th, 2018) of commercial biogas technology training courses in Cambodia under the support of the United Nations Industrial Development Organization, which has effectively extended related training programs. In this way, technical exchanges, achievement demonstrations, enterprise promotion, and experience sharing for students from the Mekong River Basin countries has been completed, and the stability and sustainability of the agricultural cooperation mechanisms of various countries was ensured.

4 Impacts

4.1 Optimizing the Structure of Agricultural Human Resources in Lancang-Mekong Countries

Based on the talent training strategy of a Chinese proverb "it is better to teach people how to fish than to give them fish", relevant Chinese organizations offered public training courses to member countries to popularize, demonstrate, and promote agricultural scientific and technological knowledge, culture, and professional skills. By integrating

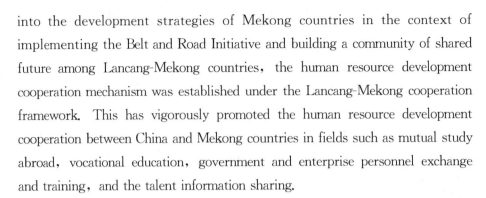
into the development strategies of Mekong countries in the context of implementing the Belt and Road Initiative and building a community of shared future among Lancang-Mekong countries, the human resource development cooperation mechanism was established under the Lancang-Mekong cooperation framework. This has vigorously promoted the human resource development cooperation between China and Mekong countries in fields such as mutual study abroad, vocational education, government and enterprise personnel exchange and training, and the talent information sharing.

4.2 Strengthening Cooperation Intention Through Training and Follow-up Communication

The trainees of Lancang-Mekong countries actively communicated with each other and promoted the mutual cooperation plan memorandum, which has improved the efficiency of communication and at the same time reached the intention of cooperation in cooperative research, capacity building, technology demonstration, communication and exchanges. Through the follow-up training and exchanges of trainees, the understanding and trust of each other have been deepened.

4.3 Raising the Awareness of a Community of Shared Future Among Lancang-Mekong Countries

During the training courses, trainees from Lancang-Mekong countries actively participated in the networking activities between Lancang-Mekong national training classes and seminars. The activities demonstrated the folk customs of various countries, enhanced mutual friendship, stimulated trainees' interest in learning and exchange enthusiasm, and were also a manifestation of the continuous innovation of Lancang-Mekong training work. This process has raised the trainees' awareness of a community of shared future among Lancang-Mekong Countries, enhanced their understanding, and deepened their friendship, which laid a solid foundation for follow-up cooperation in agricultural fields among Lancang-

Mekong countries.

5　Difficulties and Challenges

5.1　The International Exchange and Cooperation Mechanism Is Not Smooth

For example, cross-border survey and technical exchanges were restricted by long distance. Some international organizations have begun to summarize cooperation projects and discuss cooperation trends through online methods, but communication activities in some areas were not sufficient. In addition, seminars encountered great resistance during the recruitment. Taking into account the approval process and training cycles of each country, plus the fact that China's foreign-related trainings have all been held during the summer holiday, there was a shortage of students. The unified and coordinated animal transportation management and disease joint prevention and control cooperation mechanism in the region was not smooth. There were certain risks and uncertainties in carrying out cross-border animal disease prevention and control cooperation and exchanges.

5.2　The Risk of Uncertainty Has Increased Significantly

Personnel may be affected by uncertain factors such as environment, disease, diet, etc. , during the training in China and overseas, which may cause safety risks.

6　Experiences

6.1　Establishing the Multi-functional Characteristics of the Industrial Cooperation Demonstration Base

A model base of "worth working with, worth looking at, and worth talking about" has been constructed to give full play to the base's talent cultivation and technological demonstration functions.

6.2 Establishing Brand Activities of Capacity Building for Grass-roots Agricultural Extension Personnel

It is necessary to plan the grassroots agricultural technology extension personnel capacity improvement and cultivation training program, and establish a long-term cooperative development mechanism to promote the sustainable development of cultivation work, and gradually form a system and build a brand.

6.3 Strengthening Management and Ensuring Training Quality

The training course should plan in advance and actively prepare during the course of teaching. It invited teaching experts and determining the visiting route. It also arranged meetings and exchanges with experts, trainees, business leaders and farmers, which improved the level of logistics services, created a good training environment, and ensured the positive effects and the quality of training.

6.4 Strengthening Contact and Broadening Cooperation Channels

It was crucial to actively coordinate the contacts between the students and their visiting enterprises and scientific research institutions to build a bridge for deepened and further cooperation. Meanwhile, the project offered the trainees the information about studying in China and scientific research, which has expanded the impact of the training and enriched the project results.

6.5 Strengthening the Follow-up Survey and Communication in the Later Stage

It is important to give full play to the positive effects of trainings and seminars. It is necessary to strengthen the follow-up exchanges and cooperation between the government and enterprises to jointly promote the food security and sustainable development of agriculture in the Lancang-Mekong region.

澜湄国家香蕉产业合作与技术示范

Banana Industry Cooperation and Technology Demonstration Among Lancang-Mekong Countries

■ 技术人员培训 / Training for Technicians

■ 指导柬埔寨农民进行香蕉抹花处理 / Guiding Cambodian Farmers to Wipe Banana Flowers

■ 柬埔寨农民采收香蕉 / Cambodian Farmers Harvesting Bananas

湄公河次区域胡椒标准化生产技术试验示范

Experiment and Demonstration of Pepper Standard Production Technology in Mekong Sub-region

■ 胡椒优良种苗标准培训 / Standard Training on Quality Pepper Seedlings

■ 提高技术水平，获得高产 / Better Techniques, Higher Yields

■ 举办胡椒标准化生产技术培训班 / Training Course on Standardized Pepper Production Techniques

澜湄橡胶树栽培技术及加工示范基地建设

Demonstration of Integration of Rubber Tree Cultivation and Processing
Technology in Lancang-Mekong Countries

■ 收集橡胶树生长和产量数据 / Gathering
Data on Rubber Tree Growth and Yield

■ 开展技术培训 / Technical Training

■ 籽苗芽接苗工厂化生产 / Large-scale Production of Mini-budding Seedling

澜湄流域国家热带农业人才培育工程

Talent Training on Tropical Agriculture for
Lancang-Mekong Countries

■ 讲授橡胶育苗知识 / Teaching the Knowledge of Rubber Seedling

■ 学员使用中国热带农业科学院研发的
电动割胶刀 / Trainees Trying the Electric
Tapping Knife Developed by the Chinese
Academy of Tropical Agricultural Sciences

■ 无人机喷药 / Pesticide Spraying by Drone

■ 在缅甸开展田间技术培训 / Field Teaching in Myanmar

■ 在越南进行水稻测产验收工作 / Rice Yield Measurement and Acceptance
in Vietnam

澜湄流域农作物主要病虫害绿色防控合作平台创建

Experiment of Cooperation Platform for Green Control of Major Crop Pests in the Lancang-Mekong River Basin

■ 在柬埔寨开展培训 / Training Course in Cambodia

■ 澜湄国家专家代表参观中国农业科学院的生防产品 / Representatives from Lancang-Mekong Countries Visited Chinese Academy of Agricultural Sciences for the Biocontrol Products

澜湄区域优质多抗豆类新品种及绿色增产增效技术集成示范

New High-quality and Multi-resistant Bean Varieties and Integrated Demonstration of Green Production and Efficiency-increasing Technologies Among Lancang-Mekong Countries

■ 在缅甸开展绿豆产业现状调查及针对性指导 / Investigation of the Current Status and Targeted Guidance for the Mung Bean Industry in Myanmar

■ 在泰国进行田间指导 / Guidance in Field in Thailand

澜湄流域香茅种植及其产业化应用技术

Lemongrass (Citronella) Planting and Its Industrialized Application Technology in the Lancang-Mekong River Basin

■ 在柬埔寨和泰国推广的香茅新品种 / New Variety of Lemongrass (Citronella) Popularized in Cambodia and Thailand

■ 香茅系列无抗饲料产品 / Lemongrass (Citronella) Antimicrobial-free Feed Products